The World of Animals: A Comprehensive Guide

Welcome to "The World of Animals: A Comprehensive Guide." This book is an exciting journey into the extraordinary diversity of animal life that inhabits our planet. From the smallest insects to the largest mammals, from the depths of the oceans to the highest mountain peaks, the animal kingdom is a realm of wonder and fascination that has captivated humans for centuries.

Animals play a crucial role in our lives and in the ecosystems that sustain us. They are a source of inspiration, companionship, and awe. Whether you are interested in the behavior of primates, the power of apex predators, the delicate beauty of butterflies, or the mysterious allure of dinosaurs, this comprehensive guide has something for everyone.

In the pages that follow, we will delve into the rich tapestry of animal life that surrounds us. We will explore the behaviors, adaptations, habitats, and interactions that define each species. From the depths of the ocean to the vastness of the savannas, we will uncover the incredible stories of survival, evolution, and coexistence that shape the animal kingdom.

As we embark on this journey, we will also reflect on the importance of understanding and conserving the world's animal species. Our planet's delicate balance relies on the intricate relationships between animals and their environments. By learning about these relationships and the challenges they face, we can better appreciate the urgency of protecting biodiversity and ensuring the future of all living creatures.

"The World of Animals: A Comprehensive Guide" is more than just a book—it is a celebration of life in all its forms. Whether you are a passionate wildlife enthusiast, a curious student, or simply someone who marvels at the wonders of nature, this guide invites you to explore, discover, and appreciate the incredible diversity that makes up our world. Join us as we embark on this adventure into the captivating realm of the animal kingdom.

Introduction: Discovering the Diversity of Animal Life
- The fascination with animals
- Importance of understanding and conserving animal species

Chapter 1: Primates: Apes & Monkeys
- Characteristics
- Behavior and social structures
- Iconic species and their habitats

Chapter 2: Ursidae: Bears
- Different bear species and their habitats
- Behavior, diet, and adaptations
- Conservation efforts and challenges

Chapter 3: Lepidoptera: Butterflies
- Anatomy and metamorphosis
- Colorful diversity and patterns
- Butterfly gardens and conservation

Chapter 4: Felidae: Cats, Lions & Tigers
- Unique traits of domestic cats, lions, and tigers

- Distinctive features of reptiles and amphibians
- Reproduction strategies and habitats
- Conservation efforts and habitat protection

Chapter 12: Wildlife and Conservation
- Biodiversity hotspots and endangered species
- Role of protected areas and conservation organizations
- Human impact on wildlife and ethical considerations

Chapter 13: Marine Life: Underwater Wonders
- Coral reefs, marine mammals, and ocean ecosystems
- Threats to marine life and coral reef conservation
- Sustainable practices for marine environment preservation

Chapter 14: Paleontology and Fossils
- The study of fossils and ancient life forms
- Notable fossil discoveries and their significance
- Contributions of paleontology to understanding Earth's history

Conclusion: Celebrating the Richness of Animal Kingdom
- Reflection on the diversity and wonder of animals
- The importance of continued exploration and conservation

Appendix: Glossary of Key Terms
- Definitions and explanations of scientific terms used throughout the book

Recommended Reading and Resources
- Suggested books, websites, and references for further exploration

The fascination with animals

The fascination with animals is a deeply ingrained aspect of human nature. From a young age, we are drawn to the captivating beauty, diversity, and mystery of the animal kingdom. Our innate curiosity about animals has led to centuries of exploration, study, and admiration of these incredible creatures. Whether it's the grace of a soaring eagle, the playfulness of a dolphin, the intricate patterns on a butterfly's wings, or the majesty of a lion's roar, animals have an uncanny ability to capture our imagination and evoke a sense of wonder.

Animals hold a unique place in our hearts and minds. They are often featured in myths, folklore, and religious beliefs, symbolizing qualities such as strength, wisdom, freedom, and even human traits. The bonds humans form with domesticated animals, such as dogs and cats, are a testament to the companionship and emotional connections that animals can provide.

Beyond their aesthetic appeal, animals also offer valuable insights into the natural world. Studying their behaviors, adaptations, and ecological roles has contributed to advancements in science, medicine, and technology. Animals serve as models for understanding evolutionary processes, genetics, and even human psychology. Their ability to survive in diverse environments and their unique biological features continue to inspire researchers and fuel our quest for knowledge.

In an increasingly urbanized and digitally connected world,

our fascination with animals persists. Wildlife documentaries, animal-themed books and movies, and virtual encounters with animals through technology continue to captivate our attention. Moreover, the urgency of conserving endangered species and protecting ecosystems highlights the critical role animals play in maintaining the balance of our planet's delicate ecosystems.

The fascination with animals is a reminder of our connection to the natural world and the importance of preserving its beauty and diversity. As we continue to learn about and appreciate the incredible array of creatures that share our planet, we deepen our understanding of the intricate web of life and our responsibility to safeguard it for future generations.

Importance of understanding and conserving animal species

Understanding and conserving animal species is of paramount importance for a variety of reasons that extend far beyond our fascination with the natural world. Here are some key reasons why understanding and conserving animal species is crucial:

1. Biodiversity: Animals are a fundamental component of Earth's biodiversity. Biodiversity encompasses the variety of life forms, ecosystems, and genetic diversity within species. Biodiverse ecosystems are more resilient and better equipped to withstand environmental changes, making them crucial for maintaining ecosystem stability and functioning.

2. Ecological Balance: Each animal species plays a specific role within its ecosystem. From pollinating plants to controlling pest populations, animals contribute to the balance and health of their habitats. The loss of even a single species can disrupt this delicate equilibrium and have cascading effects throughout the ecosystem.

3. Human Well-being: Many animal species provide direct benefits to humans. From providing food and medicine to contributing to recreational activities like bird-watching and ecotourism, animals enhance our quality of life. Understanding and conserving these species ensures the sustainability of these resources.

4. Scientific Discovery: Animals offer valuable insights into various scientific fields, including biology,

ecology, genetics, and behavior. Studying animals provides a window into the intricacies of life and evolution, leading to advancements in medical research, genetics, and even technology.

5. Conservation of Ecosystem Services: Healthy ecosystems provide essential services such as clean water, air purification, soil fertility, and climate regulation. These services are essential for human survival and well-being, and conserving animal species is integral to maintaining these services.

6. Cultural and Aesthetic Value: Animals hold cultural significance for many societies around the world. They are often featured in art, literature, folklore, and religious practices. The loss of iconic or culturally significant species can have profound impacts on cultural identity and heritage.

7. Ethical Considerations: Animals are sentient beings with their own needs and capacities for experiencing pleasure and suffering. Recognizing their intrinsic value and treating them with respect is not only ethically important but also contributes to a more compassionate society.

8. Genetic Diversity: Animals contain a wealth of genetic diversity that can be harnessed for agriculture, medicine, and other applications. Preserving this diversity is critical for adapting to changing environmental conditions and addressing future challenges.

9. Indicator Species: Some animal species are sensitive to environmental changes and serve as indicators of ecosystem health. Monitoring these species can provide early warnings of environmental degradation and help guide conservation efforts.

10. Conservation Legacy: Ensuring the survival of animal species for future generations is a matter of intergenerational equity. We have a responsibility to

pass on a world rich in biodiversity and natural beauty to our children and grandchildren.

In an era of rapid environmental change, habitat loss, pollution, and climate change, the importance of understanding and conserving animal species cannot be overstated. It requires collaboration among scientists, policymakers, communities, and individuals to protect the intricate web of life that sustains us all.

Primates: Apes & Monkeys

Primates are a diverse group of mammals that include both apes and monkeys. They belong to the order Primates, which is characterized by their advanced cognitive abilities, flexible limbs, and forward-facing eyes. Primates have adapted to various habitats, ranging from tropical rainforests to savannas, and they can be found on nearly every continent.

Apes: Apes are a subgroup of primates known for their high level of intelligence and complex social behaviors. They are larger and more closely related to humans than monkeys. There are two main families of apes: the great apes and the lesser apes.

1. **Great Apes:**
   - **Chimpanzees:** Chimpanzees are our closest living relatives. They are known for their tool use, social structures, and sophisticated communication.
   - **Gorillas:** Gorillas are the largest primates and are divided into two species: the eastern gorilla and the western gorilla. They live in groups led by a dominant silverback male.
   - **Orangutans:** Orangutans are known for their solitary and arboreal lifestyle. They are found in the rainforests of Borneo and Sumatra and are highly endangered.
2. **Lesser Apes:**
   - **Gibbons:** Gibbons are smaller apes known for their acrobatic abilities and distinctive calls. They are found in Southeast Asia and are monogamous animals.

Monkeys: Monkeys are a diverse group of primates with various sizes, behaviors, and habitats. They can be further divided into two groups: New World monkeys and Old World monkeys.

1. **New World Monkeys:**
   - **Spider Monkeys:** Spider monkeys are known for their long limbs and prehensile tail, which they use to swing from tree to tree.
   - **Howler Monkeys:** Howler monkeys are recognized for their loud vocalizations, which can be heard from long distances in the rainforest.
   - **Capuchin Monkeys:** Capuchin monkeys are known for their intelligence and tool use. They are often seen using sticks and stones to access food.
   - **Squirrel Monkeys:** Squirrel monkeys are small and agile monkeys with a high energy level. They live in large groups and are found in Central and South America.
2. **Old World Monkeys:**
   - **Baboons:** Baboons are known for their complex social structures and adaptability to various habitats, including grasslands and forests.
   - **Macaques:** Macaques are found in a wide range of habitats and are known for their diverse behaviors, from grooming rituals to complex social interactions.
   - **Mandrills:** Mandrills are colorful monkeys with distinctive facial markings. They live in the rainforests of Central and West Africa.

Primates, including both apes and monkeys, play important ecological roles as seed dispersers and pollinators in their ecosystems. They also offer valuable insights into the evolution of intelligence, social behaviors, and communication. However, many primate species are threatened by habitat loss, poaching, and other human activities. Conservation efforts are crucial to ensure the survival of these fascinating and important creatures.

Characteristics

While apes and monkeys are both primates, they have distinct characteristics that set them apart:

Apes:

- Larger in size compared to monkeys.
- Lack a tail.
- Have a more upright posture and are capable of walking on two legs (bipedalism).
- Display more complex cognitive abilities and problem-solving skills.
- Have larger brains relative to body size compared to monkeys.
- Tend to have longer lifespans.
- Generally have more social and cooperative behaviors.
- Include some species (chimpanzees, bonobos, gorillas) that are genetically closer to humans.

Monkeys:

- Generally smaller in size compared to apes.
- Many species have a prehensile tail for grasping and holding onto objects.
- Often walk on four legs (quadrupedalism) or climb trees.
- Have a variety of cognitive abilities and social behaviors, but may not be as advanced as apes.
- May have smaller brains relative to body size compared to apes.

- Tend to have shorter lifespans compared to some apes.
- Display a range of social behaviors, from solitary to highly social.

Overall, the classification and characteristics of apes and monkeys reflect their evolutionary history and adaptations to different ecological niches. The study of these primate groups provides insights into the diversity of life forms, the development of complex behaviors, and the shared ancestry between humans and other primates.

Behavior and social structures

Behavior and Social Structures of Apes and Monkeys: Apes and monkeys exhibit a wide range of behaviors and social structures that are shaped by their evolutionary history, ecological niches, and environmental challenges. While there is variability within each group, certain patterns can be observed in their behavior and social interactions:

Apes: Apes, including gorillas, chimpanzees, bonobos, and orangutans, are known for their complex behaviors and social structures.

- **Social Structures:** Apes generally live in social groups that vary in size and composition. Gorillas live in stable groups led by a dominant silverback male, with multiple females and their offspring. Chimpanzees and bonobos live in multi-male, multi-female communities with complex hierarchies. Orangutans are more solitary, with males having overlapping territories and occasional interactions with females.
- **Tool Use:** Some species of apes, particularly chimpanzees, are known for their tool-using behaviors. They use sticks, leaves, and other objects to obtain food or for other purposes.
- **Communication:** Apes communicate through vocalizations, body language, and facial expressions. They can convey emotions, intentions, and warnings through these forms of communication.
- **Cognition and Problem Solving:** Apes have demonstrated advanced cognitive abilities, including the ability to solve complex problems, use tools, and

even engage in planning and cooperation.

- **Cultural Behaviors:** Some populations of chimpanzees and other apes show evidence of cultural behaviors, where certain behaviors are passed down through generations and vary between different groups.

Monkeys: Monkeys, including both Old World and New World monkeys, also exhibit diverse behaviors and social structures.

- **Social Structures:** Monkey social structures vary widely based on species. Old World monkeys often live in larger social groups with complex hierarchies. New World monkeys may live in smaller groups or family units.
- **Communication:** Monkeys use a variety of vocalizations, gestures, and body language to communicate with each other. Some species have distinct calls for different predators or threats.
- **Foraging and Feeding:** Monkeys are opportunistic feeders and have adapted to various diets, including fruits, leaves, insects, and small vertebrates. They use different strategies for finding and obtaining food.
- **Reproductive Strategies:** Monkeys have diverse reproductive behaviors, including various mating systems, courtship rituals, and infant care strategies.
- **Play Behavior:** Many monkey species engage in play behaviors, which help them develop social and cognitive skills.
- **Grooming:** Grooming is an important social behavior among monkeys. It helps build social bonds, reduce tension, and maintain hygiene within the group.

Commonalities and Differences: Both apes and monkeys exhibit social behaviors that contribute to their survival and reproduction. However, apes generally display more complex cognitive abilities, including tool use, problem-solving, and cultural transmission. Monkeys exhibit a wide range of behaviors adapted to their ecological niches and social dynamics. The study of their behaviors and social structures provides valuable insights into the evolution of sociality, cooperation, communication, and cognition within the primate order.

Iconic species and their habitats

Iconic Species of Apes & Monkeys and Their Habitats:

Apes and monkeys are diverse and fascinating creatures that inhabit various ecosystems around the world. Here are some iconic species of apes and monkeys, along with their habitats:

1. **Chimpanzee (Pan troglodytes):**
   - **Habitat:** Chimpanzees are found in the tropical rainforests and woodlands of central and West Africa.
2. **Gorilla (Gorilla spp.):**
   - **Habitat:** Gorillas inhabit the forests of central and East Africa, including rainforests, montane forests, and swamp forests.
3. **Orangutan (Pongo spp.):**
   - **Habitat:** Orangutans are native to the rainforests of Borneo and Sumatra, where they live in the canopy of tropical forests.
4. **Howler Monkey (Alouatta spp.):**
   - **Habitat:** Howler monkeys are found in the forests of Central and South America, including rainforests, mangroves, and deciduous forests.
5. **Capuchin Monkey (Cebus spp.):**
   - **Habitat:** Capuchin monkeys inhabit a variety of habitats in Central and South America, including rainforests, savannas, and mangroves.
6. **Japanese Macaque (Macaca fuscata):**
   - **Habitat:** Japanese macaques, also known as

snow monkeys, live in various habitats across Japan, including forests, mountains, and hot springs.

7. **Golden Lion Tamarin (Leontopithecus rosalia):**
   - **Habitat:** Golden lion tamarins are endemic to the Atlantic coastal rainforests of Brazil.

8. **Mandrill (Mandrillus sphinx):**
   - **Habitat:** Mandrills are found in the rainforests and dense woodlands of central Africa.

9. **Spider Monkey (Ateles spp.):**
   - **Habitat:** Spider monkeys inhabit the rainforests of Central and South America, where they use their long limbs and prehensile tails to swing through trees.

10. **Bonobo (Pan paniscus):**
    - **Habitat:** Bonobos are found in the dense tropical rainforests of the Democratic Republic of Congo.

These iconic species of apes and monkeys are not only important for the ecosystems they inhabit but also hold cultural and scientific significance. Studying their behaviors, social structures, and interactions with their environments can provide insights into both their own species and broader topics in ecology and biology. Protecting their habitats and ensuring their survival is essential for maintaining biodiversity and the health of our planet's ecosystems.

Ursidae: Bears

Ursidae: Bears

Bears are charismatic and iconic mammals that belong to the family Ursidae. These large and powerful creatures are known for their diverse behaviors, habitats, and roles in ecosystems. Here's an overview of bears and their characteristics:

1. **Characteristics:**
   - Bears are mammals characterized by their stocky bodies, large size, and plantigrade feet (walking on the soles of their feet).
   - They have a strong sense of smell and excellent hearing, which aids them in finding food and detecting potential threats.
   - Bears have long, curved claws that they use for various activities, including digging for food, climbing, and defending themselves.

2. **Habitats:**
   - Bears inhabit a range of habitats, from forests and mountains to tundras and swamps, depending on the species.
   - Different species of bears are adapted to specific environments. For example, polar bears are found in the Arctic region, while black bears can be found in forests across North America.

3. **Behavior:**
   - Bears are known for their wide range of behaviors, including foraging, hunting, fishing, and hibernating.

- Some bears, like the grizzly bear, are known for their fishing skills, catching salmon during the spawning season.
- Many bears are solitary animals, while others, like the American black bear, may tolerate the presence of other bears in their territories.

4. **Species Diversity:**
   - The Ursidae family includes several species of bears, each with unique adaptations and characteristics:
     - Polar Bear (Ursus maritimus)
     - Grizzly Bear (Ursus arctos horribilis)
     - American Black Bear (Ursus americanus)
     - Brown Bear (Ursus arctos)
     - Giant Panda (Ailuropoda melanoleuca)
     - And more.

5. **Conservation Status:**
   - Many bear species are listed as vulnerable or endangered due to habitat loss, poaching, and other threats.
   - Conservation efforts aim to protect bears and their habitats, promote coexistence with humans, and raise awareness about the importance of these apex predators in maintaining healthy ecosystems.

6. **Cultural Significance:**
   - Bears have cultural significance in various societies and mythologies around the world.
   - They appear in stories, legends, and religious beliefs, often symbolizing strength, wisdom, and power.

7. **Human Interactions:**
   - Bears have sometimes come into conflict with humans due to habitat encroachment and food scarcity, leading to incidents of bear-

human interactions.

- Efforts are made to educate communities about bear behavior, implement responsible practices in bear habitats, and minimize potential conflicts.

Bears are a vital part of our natural world, contributing to ecological balance and biodiversity. Their behaviors, habitats, and interactions with their environments provide valuable insights into the natural world and highlight the importance of preserving their habitats and coexisting with these majestic creatures.

Different bear species and their habitats

Different Bear Species and Their Habitats

Bears are found in various parts of the world, adapting to a wide range of habitats that suit their specific needs and preferences. Here's an overview of different bear species and their respective habitats:

1. **Polar Bear (Ursus maritimus):**
   - Habitat: Arctic regions, including sea ice, coastlines, and islands.
   - Adaptations: Polar bears are adapted to cold environments and are excellent swimmers. They primarily rely on sea ice for hunting seals.
2. **Grizzly Bear (Ursus arctos horribilis):**
   - Habitat: North America, including forests, mountains, and tundras.
   - Adaptations: Grizzly bears have a varied diet, including plants, berries, fish, and small mammals. They are known for their fishing skills during salmon runs.
3. **American Black Bear (Ursus americanus):**
   - Habitat: North America, including forests, swamps, and grasslands.
   - Adaptations: American black bears are versatile omnivores, eating a wide range of foods such as fruits, nuts, insects, and small mammals.
4. **Brown Bear (Ursus arctos):**
   - Habitat: Europe, Asia, and North America,

including forests, tundras, and mountains.

- Adaptations: Brown bears have varying diets based on their habitats, including fish, vegetation, and small mammals.

5. **Giant Panda (Ailuropoda melanoleuca):**
   - Habitat: Mountainous regions of China.
   - Adaptations: Giant pandas are primarily herbivores, feeding on bamboo. Their diet has shaped their digestive and physiological adaptations.

6. **Sloth Bear (Melursus ursinus):**
   - Habitat: Forested areas of South Asia.
   - Adaptations: Sloth bears primarily feed on insects, using their specialized lips to extract termites and ants from their nests.

7. **Andean Bear (Tremarctos ornatus):**
   - Habitat: Andean regions of South America.
   - Adaptations: Andean bears are skilled climbers and predominantly consume plant material, such as fruits and bromeliads.

8. **Sun Bear (Helarctos malayanus):**
   - Habitat: Southeast Asia, including tropical rainforests.
   - Adaptations: Sun bears are known for their long tongues, which they use to extract insects and honey from trees.

9. **Asiatic Black Bear (Ursus thibetanus):**
   - Habitat: Asia, including forests and mountains.
   - Adaptations: Asiatic black bears have a varied diet, consisting of fruits, insects, small mammals, and even larger prey.

10. **Spectacled Bear (Tremarctos ornatus):**
    - Habitat: South America, including the Andes mountains and cloud forests.
    - Adaptations: Spectacled bears are primarily

herbivores, consuming a variety of plants, fruits, and vegetation.

Each bear species has evolved to thrive in its specific habitat, utilizing various adaptations and behaviors to secure food, find shelter, and reproduce. The diversity of bear habitats reflects their incredible ability to occupy a wide range of ecosystems across the globe.

Behavior, diet, and adaptations

Behavior, Diet, and Adaptations of Bears

Bears are fascinating creatures known for their diverse behaviors, diets, and remarkable adaptations that enable them to survive in various habitats. Here's an overview of their behavior, diet, and key adaptations:

Behavior:

- **Solitary Nature:** Most bear species are solitary animals, except during mating or when females have cubs.
- **Territorial Behavior:** Bears mark their territories through scent marking and vocalizations to avoid confrontations with other bears.
- **Hibernation:** Many bear species hibernate during the winter to conserve energy when food is scarce.
- **Parental Care:** Female bears exhibit strong maternal instincts and protect and care for their cubs for an extended period.

Diet:

- **Omnivorous:** Bears are omnivores, consuming a variety of foods depending on their habitat.
- **Plant Matter:** They eat vegetation such as berries, fruits, nuts, and plants.
- **Animal Protein:** Some bears are skilled hunters and catch prey such as fish, seals, and small mammals.
- **Insects:** Bears, like the grizzly and panda, eat insects as a significant part of their diet.

- **Scavenging:** They are opportunistic scavengers, feeding on carrion and human food sources.

Adaptations:

- **Diverse Dentition:** Bears have varying dental adaptations based on their diet, from flat molars for grinding plant matter to sharp teeth for hunting.
- **Strong Claws:** Their sharp claws help them dig for food, excavate dens, and climb trees.
- **Keen Sense of Smell:** Bears have an excellent sense of smell used for locating food and detecting danger.
- **Thick Fur and Fat Reserves:** Their fur and fat layers provide insulation and energy storage, especially during hibernation.
- **Hibernation Physiology:** Bears' metabolic rate drops during hibernation, allowing them to survive on stored fat reserves.
- **Swimming and Climbing:** Species like polar bears are strong swimmers, while others, like black bears, are adept climbers.

These behaviors, diets, and adaptations have allowed bears to inhabit a diverse range of ecosystems, from dense forests to icy polar regions. The ability to adjust their behavior and diet to their surroundings demonstrates their remarkable ability to survive and thrive in a changing world.

Conservation efforts and challenges

Conservation Efforts and Challenges for Bears

Bears play an essential role in maintaining ecosystem health, and their conservation is crucial to preserving biodiversity. However, they face various challenges that threaten their populations. Conservation efforts aim to address these challenges and ensure the survival of bear species worldwide. Here's an overview of conservation efforts and challenges for bears:

Conservation Efforts:

- **Protected Areas:** Establishing and managing protected areas helps conserve bear habitats and provide safe spaces for them to live and reproduce.
- **Habitat Restoration:** Restoration projects focus on restoring degraded habitats and creating corridors for bears to move between fragmented areas.
- **Anti-Poaching Measures:** Enforcing strict anti-poaching laws and increasing patrols help combat illegal hunting and trade of bear parts.
- **Human-Bear Conflict Management:** Implementing strategies to reduce conflicts between bears and humans, such as using bear-proof containers for food storage, prevents negative interactions.
- **Education and Outreach:** Public awareness campaigns educate communities about the importance of bears and their role in ecosystems.
- **Research and Monitoring:** Conducting research on bear populations, behavior, and ecology informs

conservation strategies and helps track population trends.

Challenges:

- **Habitat Loss and Fragmentation:** Urbanization, deforestation, and development result in loss and fragmentation of bear habitats, limiting their range and resources.
- **Poaching and Illegal Trade:** Bears are hunted for their body parts, used in traditional medicine and sold on the black market, threatening their populations.
- **Climate Change:** Climate change impacts bear habitats, altering food availability and contributing to habitat loss due to rising temperatures and changing ecosystems.
- **Human-Bear Conflict:** Bears that come into contact with humans may face conflicts leading to their injury or death as a result of perceived threats.
- **Disease Outbreaks:** Bears are vulnerable to diseases that can spread through populations, impacting their health and survival.
- **Lack of Awareness:** Many people are unaware of the importance of bears and the threats they face, hindering conservation efforts.

Efforts to conserve bears involve collaboration among governments, organizations, researchers, and local communities. Conservation initiatives address these challenges by promoting sustainable practices, protecting habitats, and raising awareness about the importance of bears in maintaining healthy ecosystems. Through these efforts, conservationists aim to secure the future of bear species and ensure their vital role in the natural world.

Lepidoptera: Butterflies

Lepidoptera: Butterflies

Butterflies, belonging to the order Lepidoptera, are among the most captivating and beloved insects in the world. Their exquisite beauty, intricate wing patterns, and remarkable life cycle have captured the imagination of people for centuries. Here's an overview of butterflies, their characteristics, life cycle, ecological significance, and conservation efforts:

Characteristics:

- Butterflies are insects characterized by their distinctive wing structures covered in tiny scales that give them their vibrant colors and patterns.
- They have a unique life cycle consisting of four stages: egg, caterpillar (larva), pupa (chrysalis), and adult butterfly.
- Butterflies have specialized mouthparts called proboscises, which they use to sip nectar from flowers.

Life Cycle:

1. **Egg:** Butterflies lay eggs on host plants, which provide food for the emerging caterpillars.
2. **Caterpillar (Larva):** The caterpillar hatches from the egg and feeds voraciously on leaves, growing and molting several times.
3. **Pupa (Chrysalis):** The caterpillar undergoes metamorphosis inside a pupa, during which its body transforms into the adult butterfly's structure.
4. **Adult Butterfly:** The fully developed butterfly emerges

from the pupa, allowing its wings to dry and expand before taking flight.

Ecological Significance:

- Butterflies play a vital role in ecosystems as pollinators, helping plants reproduce by transferring pollen from one flower to another.
- They are indicators of environmental health and biodiversity. Changes in butterfly populations can reflect changes in ecosystems.
- Butterflies are a food source for many predators, contributing to the intricate web of life in ecosystems.

Conservation Efforts:

- **Habitat Protection:** Protecting natural habitats, such as meadows, forests, and wetlands, is crucial for the survival of butterfly species.
- **Native Plant Restoration:** Planting native host plants helps provide food for caterpillars and nectar sources for adult butterflies.
- **Reducing Pesticide Use:** Reducing or eliminating the use of pesticides helps preserve butterfly populations and their habitats.
- **Creating Butterfly Gardens:** Creating gardens with nectar-rich flowers and host plants provides habitats for butterflies in urban areas.
- **Education and Outreach:** Raising awareness about the importance of butterflies and their conservation fosters public support for their protection.

Butterflies face threats such as habitat loss, climate change, pollution, and pesticide use. Conservation efforts focus on mitigating these threats to ensure the survival of diverse butterfly species. By valuing and protecting these delicate insects, we contribute to the health of ecosystems and appreciate the beauty they bring to the natural world.

Anatomy and metamorphosis

Anatomy and Metamorphosis of Butterflies

The fascinating world of butterflies is characterized not only by their vibrant colors and graceful flight but also by their unique anatomy and remarkable metamorphosis. Understanding their anatomy and life cycle provides insights into the intricacies of these captivating insects:

Anatomy:

1. **Head:** The butterfly's head contains compound eyes, antennae, and mouthparts. Their large compound eyes enable them to detect movement and colors.
2. **Thorax:** The thorax houses the powerful muscles that control the wings' movement. It is also where the six legs are attached.
3. **Abdomen:** The abdomen contains vital organs such as the digestive and reproductive systems. It may also store fat and contribute to the butterfly's overall body shape.
4. **Wings:** The butterfly's most iconic feature, the wings, are covered in tiny, overlapping scales that give them their color and pattern. The scales create the delicate appearance of the wings.

Metamorphosis: The life cycle of a butterfly involves a complete metamorphosis, a process of distinct stages leading from egg to adult:

1. **Egg:** A butterfly lays eggs on host plants. The egg stage can vary in duration depending on environmental

conditions.

2. **Caterpillar (Larva):** The hatched caterpillar emerges from the egg and spends its time eating and growing. It undergoes multiple molts, shedding its exoskeleton to accommodate its increasing size.

3. **Pupa (Chrysalis):** The caterpillar attaches itself to a surface and undergoes metamorphosis inside a chrysalis. Inside, the caterpillar's body transforms into the adult butterfly's structure. This process may take days to weeks.

4. **Adult Butterfly:** Once metamorphosis is complete, the adult butterfly emerges from the chrysalis. Its wings are initially soft and crumpled but quickly expand and dry, allowing the butterfly to fly.

Metamorphosis serves various purposes for butterflies. The caterpillar stage is focused on growth and feeding, while the pupa stage facilitates the transformation of the caterpillar's body into that of a butterfly. This intricate process is a testament to the adaptability and complexity of the natural world.

The remarkable anatomy and metamorphosis of butterflies highlight their unique adaptations for survival and reproduction. From their compound eyes to their delicate wings, butterflies are a marvel of nature's design. Their life cycle, characterized by complete metamorphosis, contributes to their ecological roles as pollinators and showcases the wonders of biological diversity.

Colorful diversity and patterns

Colorful Diversity and Patterns in Butterflies

One of the most enchanting aspects of butterflies is their stunning and diverse array of colors and patterns. These visual features serve various purposes, from attracting mates to providing camouflage and warning signals. The world of butterflies is a canvas of colors, shapes, and patterns that reflects their evolutionary history and ecological roles:

1. Camouflage and Mimicry:

- **Cryptic Coloration:** Some butterflies have evolved patterns that help them blend seamlessly into their surroundings, making them difficult for predators to spot.
- **Mimicry:** Certain butterfly species mimic the appearance of toxic or unpalatable species to deter predators from attacking them. This phenomenon, known as Batesian mimicry, showcases a harmless species imitating a harmful one.

2. Warning Signals and Aposematism:

- **Bright Colors:** Many butterflies display bold and vibrant colors as a warning to predators that they are toxic or unpalatable. This defense mechanism, known as aposematism, warns potential predators to avoid consuming them.
- **Müllerian Mimicry:** Some unrelated toxic butterfly species have evolved similar color patterns to reinforce the warning signals. This mutual mimicry benefits all

the species involved.

3. Sexual Selection:

- **Sexual Dimorphism:** In some species, males and females display different colors and patterns, which can play a role in mate selection. Males may use their bright colors to attract females, while females' patterns might help them select a suitable mate.

4. Habitat and Ecology:

- **Habitat Specificity:** Butterflies often exhibit colors and patterns that are adapted to their specific habitats. This enables them to blend in and avoid predators, as well as find food sources.
- **Thermoregulation:** Dark-colored butterflies can absorb more heat from the sun, aiding in thermoregulation and enhancing their activity levels.

5. UV Reflectance and Communication:

- **Ultraviolet Colors:** Some butterfly patterns are visible only in ultraviolet light, which plays a role in communication between butterflies and mate selection. Males, for instance, may have UV-reflective patches that attract females.

6. Geographic Variation and Speciation:

- **Geographic Patterns:** Butterfly colors and patterns can vary geographically within a species, leading to unique regional variations. This variation can contribute to the process of speciation.

Butterflies' colors and patterns are the result of complex interactions between genetics, environmental factors, and evolutionary pressures. They exemplify the diverse strategies that animals have developed to survive, reproduce, and thrive in their respective ecosystems. Whether it's a cryptic caterpillar or a boldly colored adult, the visual beauty of butterflies serves as a reminder of nature's creativity and the intricate web of life on Earth.

Butterfly gardens and conservation

Butterfly Gardens and Conservation

Butterfly gardens play a vital role in the conservation of these delicate and fascinating insects. By creating suitable habitats, providing food sources, and raising awareness about butterfly species, butterfly gardens contribute to the preservation of these important pollinators and their ecosystems:

1. Habitat Restoration:

- Butterfly gardens provide essential habitat for local butterfly populations, especially in urban and developed areas where natural habitats are dwindling.
- Native plants that are well-suited to the local climate and soil conditions are often used in butterfly gardens to attract specific butterfly species.

2. Nectar Sources:

- Butterfly gardens offer a variety of nectar-rich flowers that serve as food sources for adult butterflies. These flowers not only provide sustenance for butterflies but also attract other pollinators like bees and hummingbirds.

3. Host Plants:

- Many butterfly species have specific host plants where they lay their eggs. These host plants provide food for caterpillars once they hatch.
- Including host plants in butterfly gardens is essential for supporting the entire life cycle of butterflies.

4. Education and Awareness:

- Butterfly gardens serve as educational tools that raise awareness about the importance of pollinators, the challenges they face, and the ways people can contribute to conservation efforts.
- Visitors to butterfly gardens can learn about the life cycle of butterflies, their behaviors, and their role in ecosystems.

5. Citizen Science:

- Butterfly gardens often encourage citizen science initiatives, where volunteers can observe and document butterfly species present in the garden. This data contributes to scientific research and conservation efforts.

6. Conservation of Endangered Species:

- Some butterfly gardens focus on providing habitat for rare and endangered butterfly species, contributing to their protection and recovery.
- These gardens may collaborate with conservation organizations to implement targeted conservation strategies.

7. Community Engagement:

- Butterfly gardens can bring together communities, schools, and local organizations to collaborate on conservation projects and promote environmental stewardship.

8. Ecotourism and Economic Benefits:

- Butterfly gardens can attract visitors and tourists interested in experiencing the beauty of butterflies up close.

- This ecotourism aspect can have positive economic impacts on local communities.

9. Supporting Biodiversity:

- Creating butterfly gardens that attract a variety of butterfly species also benefits other pollinators and wildlife, contributing to overall biodiversity.

In a world where habitat loss, pesticide use, and climate change threaten butterfly populations, butterfly gardens serve as oases of refuge and regeneration. They provide a space for people to connect with nature, observe the intricate lives of butterflies, and contribute to the broader effort to conserve these beloved insects and the ecosystems they inhabit.

Felidae: Cats, Lions & Tigers

Felidae: Cats, Lions & Tigers

The Felidae family includes a diverse group of carnivorous mammals known for their grace, agility, and predatory abilities. Within this family, there are various species, each with its own unique characteristics and behaviors:

1. Cats (Domestic Cats):

- Domestic cats (Felis catus) are beloved pets that have been companions to humans for thousands of years.
- They display a range of behaviors, from playful antics to hunting instincts.
- Domestic cats are known for their grooming habits, sharp retractable claws, and keen senses.

2. Lions (Panthera leo):

- Lions are social animals that live in prides, consisting of multiple related females, their offspring, and a few males.
- Male lions have distinctive manes and are often seen as symbols of strength and majesty.
- Lions are apex predators and their cooperative hunting strategies make them formidable hunters.

3. Tigers (Panthera tigris):

- Tigers are the largest of all cats and are known for their distinctive orange coats with dark stripes.
- They are solitary animals that are highly adapted for stealthy hunting.

- Tigers are endangered, with habitat loss and poaching being significant threats to their survival.

4. Behavior and Adaptations:

- All members of the Felidae family are carnivores with sharp claws and teeth designed for capturing and consuming prey.
- Cats have excellent night vision and acute hearing, which make them effective predators.
- Tigers are powerful swimmers and are known to inhabit regions with water sources.

5. Conservation Concerns:

- While domestic cats are widespread and cared for as pets, many wild cat species, including lions and tigers, are facing threats to their survival.
- Habitat loss, poaching for body parts, and conflicts with humans are major challenges for wild cat populations.

6. Ecological Importance:

- Wild cats play a crucial role in maintaining ecological balance by controlling prey populations, thereby preventing overgrazing and maintaining ecosystem health.

7. Cultural Significance:

- Cats have been revered in various cultures throughout history, symbolizing attributes such as independence, mystery, and guardianship.
- Lions and tigers are often depicted as symbols of strength, courage, and nobility in human culture.

8. Conservation Efforts:

- Conservation organizations are working to protect and

> restore habitat for wild cat species.
> - Anti-poaching efforts and initiatives to reduce human-wildlife conflicts are critical for their survival.

From the domestic cats that share our homes to the majestic lions and tigers that roam the wild, the members of the Felidae family capture our imagination and inspire awe. Understanding their behavior, habitat needs, and conservation challenges is essential for ensuring the survival of these iconic and enigmatic creatures for generations to come.

Unique traits of domestic cats, lions, and tigers

Unique Traits of Domestic Cats, Lions, and Tigers

Domestic cats, lions, and tigers belong to the same family, Felidae, but they exhibit distinct characteristics and behaviors that make each species unique:

Domestic Cats (Felis catus):

1. **Variety of Breeds:** Domestic cats come in various breeds, each with its own physical traits and personalities. From the playful and active Abyssinian to the fluffy and laid-back Persian, domestic cats display a wide range of appearances and temperaments.
2. **Independence:** Domestic cats are known for their independent nature. They can groom themselves, use a litter box, and entertain themselves with toys.
3. **Communication:** Cats communicate through various vocalizations, such as meowing, purring, and hissing, as well as through body language like tail position and ear orientation.
4. **Agility:** Domestic cats are excellent climbers and jumpers. They have retractable claws that allow them to grip surfaces and pounce on prey.
5. **Hunting Instinct:** Even though domestic cats are often well-fed by their owners, they retain their instinctual hunting behavior, often chasing and "playing" with toys to mimic hunting.

6. **Grooming:** Cats are meticulous groomers. They use their rough tongues to clean their fur and remove dirt and loose hair.

Lions (Panthera leo):

1. **Social Structure:** Unlike most other cats, lions are social animals that live in groups called prides. A pride usually consists of related females, their cubs, and a few males.
2. **Manes:** Male lions are easily recognizable by their impressive manes, which vary in color and size. The mane is believed to play a role in attracting mates and asserting dominance.
3. **Cooperative Hunting:** Lions often hunt together in groups, which increases their chances of capturing larger prey. Their collaborative hunting techniques involve surrounding and ambushing the target.
4. **Territorial Behavior:** Male lions mark their territories with scent markings and vocalizations. They defend their pride's territory against other prides and intruders.
5. **Vocalizations:** Lions have a range of vocalizations, including roars that can be heard from long distances. Roaring serves to establish territory and communicate with pride members.

Tigers (Panthera tigris):

1. **Size and Strength:** Tigers are the largest cats in the world, known for their powerful build and strength. They have muscular bodies and large paws equipped with sharp claws.
2. **Distinctive Coat:** Tigers have a distinct orange coat with black stripes that provide effective camouflage in their natural habitats, such as grasslands and forests.
3. **Solitary Behavior:** Tigers are solitary animals, except

during mating and when a mother is raising her cubs. They establish and defend territories from other tigers.

4. **Swimming Ability:** Unlike many other cats, tigers are good swimmers and are known to enjoy bathing and cooling off in water bodies.

5. **Stalking and Ambushing:** Tigers are skilled stalkers and ambush predators. They rely on their camouflage and patience to get close to their prey before launching a sudden attack.

6. **Diverse Habitat Range:** Tigers inhabit a range of habitats, including mangrove swamps, grasslands, and rainforests. Different subspecies are adapted to specific environments.

While all three species share the common traits of the Felidae family, their unique characteristics have evolved to suit their respective lifestyles, habitats, and ecological roles. Understanding these traits is essential for appreciating the diversity and complexity of the feline world.

Hunting strategies and social behaviors

Hunting Strategies and Social Behaviors

Each of these feline species - domestic cats, lions, and tigers - has distinct hunting strategies and social behaviors that have evolved to suit their ecological niches and lifestyles:

Domestic Cats:

- **Hunting:** Domestic cats are solitary hunters, often using their agility and stealth to stalk and pounce on prey. They primarily target smaller animals such as rodents, birds, and insects.
- **Play Behavior:** Play behavior in domestic cats mimics hunting behavior. Pouncing on toys, stalking imaginary prey, and batting at objects are ways for domestic cats to engage their natural instincts.
- **Territorial Behavior:** While domestic cats may have some overlapping territories, they are generally solitary animals that mark their territory with scent markings.

Lions:

- **Cooperative Hunting:** Lions are social animals that hunt cooperatively in groups called prides. They often use their teamwork and numbers to bring down larger prey such as buffalo, zebras, and wildebeests.
- **Role Differentiation:** Within a lion pride, females often participate in group hunts while the males focus on protecting the territory and pride members.
- **Sharing Food:** Once a kill is made, lions share the food

with each other, prioritizing the young and injured members of the pride.

- **Social Bonding:** Lions in a pride engage in social interactions such as grooming, nuzzling, and playing, which helps to strengthen the bonds between pride members.

Tigers:

- **Solitary Hunting:** Tigers are solitary hunters that rely on stealth and camouflage to approach their prey closely before launching an ambush.
- **Preferred Prey:** Tigers are known to have a preference for larger ungulates such as deer, wild boars, and cattle. They also have been known to hunt smaller animals if larger prey is scarce.
- **Stalking and Ambushing:** Tigers are excellent stalkers, using vegetation and cover to hide their approach until they are close enough to pounce on their prey.
- **Territorial Behavior:** Tigers establish and defend territories that encompass their preferred prey resources. They use scent markings and vocalizations to communicate their presence and boundaries.

While domestic cats, lions, and tigers share the fundamental traits of carnivorous predators, their hunting strategies and social behaviors are tailored to their specific lifestyles. Domestic cats have adapted to life as companions, while lions and tigers have evolved complex social structures and specialized hunting techniques that optimize their chances of survival in their respective environments.

Conservation status and efforts

Conservation Status and Efforts

The conservation status of domestic cats, lions, and tigers varies significantly due to their different ecological roles and habitats. Here's an overview of their conservation status and ongoing efforts to protect them:

Domestic Cats:

- Conservation Status: Domestic cats are not considered threatened or endangered as a species. However, some domestic cat populations, particularly feral cats, can have negative impacts on local wildlife populations.
- Conservation Efforts: Efforts to address the impact of domestic cats on wildlife include promoting responsible pet ownership, spaying/neutering programs for feral cats, and raising awareness about the importance of keeping cats indoors to prevent predation on wildlife.

Lions:

- Conservation Status: Lions are listed as "Vulnerable" by the International Union for Conservation of Nature (IUCN). Their populations have declined due to habitat loss, human-wildlife conflict, and poaching.
- Conservation Efforts: Conservation organizations work to protect lion habitats, mitigate human-wildlife conflicts, and combat poaching. Community-based conservation initiatives engage local communities in lion conservation efforts.

Tigers:

- Conservation Status: Tigers are classified as "Endangered" by the IUCN. Their populations have been drastically reduced due to habitat loss, poaching for their body parts, and conflicts with humans.
- Conservation Efforts: Many organizations are focused on protecting tiger habitats, preventing poaching, and raising awareness about the importance of tiger conservation. Initiatives include strengthening anti-poaching measures and promoting sustainable development practices.

Conservation efforts for all three species involve a combination of habitat protection, legal measures, community engagement, research, and education. While domestic cats primarily benefit from responsible pet ownership, lions and tigers require more comprehensive strategies due to their status as large apex predators. International cooperation and local involvement are essential to ensuring the survival of these iconic species and maintaining the health of their ecosystems.

Mesozoic Era: Dinosaurs

Mesozoic Era: Dinosaurs

The Mesozoic Era, often referred to as the "Age of Dinosaurs," spanned from approximately 252 million years ago to 66 million years ago. During this era, dinosaurs evolved, diversified, and dominated terrestrial ecosystems. The Mesozoic Era is divided into three major periods: the Triassic, Jurassic, and Cretaceous periods. Here's an overview of dinosaurs during each period:

Triassic Period (252-201 million years ago):

- Early Dinosaurs: The Triassic marked the emergence of the first dinosaurs, which were relatively small and bipedal. Examples include Herrerasaurus and Eoraptor.
- Diversification: By the late Triassic, dinosaurs had diversified into various forms, including carnivores and herbivores. Archosaurs, the group that includes dinosaurs, crocodiles, and birds, were prominent during this period.

Jurassic Period (201-145 million years ago):

- Evolution of Large Dinosaurs: The Jurassic saw the evolution of larger dinosaurs, including some of the most iconic species. Sauropods like Brachiosaurus and Diplodocus were massive herbivores, while theropods like Allosaurus and Ceratosaurus were carnivorous predators.
- Rise of Theropods: Theropod dinosaurs, characterized by their bipedal stance and sharp teeth, were diverse

and ecologically successful during the Jurassic. Some early birds also evolved from small theropods.

Cretaceous Period (145-66 million years ago):

- Continued Diversification: The Cretaceous saw further diversification of dinosaurs. Large herbivorous dinosaurs like Triceratops and hadrosaurs were common, while theropods continued to evolve into various forms.
- Avian Dinosaurs: By the Late Cretaceous, some theropods had evolved into birds with feathers, beaks, and hollow bones. These early birds shared characteristics with their dinosaur ancestors.
- End-Cretaceous Extinction: The Cretaceous-Paleogene (K-Pg) extinction event, 66 million years ago, marked the end of the Mesozoic Era. This event led to the extinction of non-avian dinosaurs, allowing mammals and other organisms to fill ecological niches.

The Mesozoic Era was a time of dynamic evolution and ecological change, with dinosaurs playing a central role in shaping terrestrial ecosystems. Fossils and paleontological discoveries continue to provide insights into the lives, behaviors, and adaptations of these ancient creatures, offering a glimpse into a world that existed millions of years ago.

Overview of different dinosaur types

Overview of Different Dinosaur Types

Dinosaurs were a diverse group of reptiles that lived during the Mesozoic Era and can be classified into several different types based on their characteristics, features, and behaviors. Here's an overview of some of the major dinosaur types:

1. **Sauropods:**
   - Characteristics: Sauropods were large, long-necked, herbivorous dinosaurs with small heads, long tails, and massive bodies. They had a quadrupedal stance.
   - Examples: Brachiosaurus, Apatosaurus (formerly known as Brontosaurus), Diplodocus, Argentinosaurus.

2. **Theropods:**
   - Characteristics: Theropods were bipedal, carnivorous dinosaurs with sharp teeth and clawed hands. They varied in size from small to large.
   - Examples: Tyrannosaurus rex, Velociraptor, Allosaurus, Spinosaurus.

3. **Ornithischians:**
   - Characteristics: Ornithischians were herbivorous dinosaurs with a unique hip structure resembling that of birds. They had various forms of beaks and teeth for grinding plant material.
   - Examples: Triceratops, Stegosaurus, Ankylosaurus, Hadrosaurs (duck-billed

dinosaurs).

4. **Ceratopsians:**
   - Characteristics: Ceratopsians were herbivorous dinosaurs with distinct frills and horns on their heads. They were often quadrupedal and had beaks for cropping vegetation.
   - Examples: Triceratops, Protoceratops, Styracosaurus.

5. **Thyreophorans:**
   - Characteristics: Thyreophorans were dinosaurs with armored plates and spikes on their bodies for defense. They could be either herbivorous or omnivorous.
   - Examples: Stegosaurus, Ankylosaurus, Scelidosaurus.

6. **Pterosaurs:**
   - Characteristics: Pterosaurs were flying reptiles and not dinosaurs, but they lived alongside them. They had wings formed by a skin membrane stretched between elongated fingers.
   - Examples: Pteranodon, Quetzalcoatlus.

7. **Avian Dinosaurs (Birds):**
   - Characteristics: Birds are the living descendants of theropod dinosaurs. They have feathers, beaks, and lay eggs. Some theropod dinosaurs evolved into early birds during the Late Jurassic and Early Cretaceous.
   - Examples: Archaeopteryx (early bird), modern birds.

It's important to note that the classification of dinosaurs is based on their anatomical features, and new discoveries and research continue to refine our understanding of their relationships and classifications. The study of dinosaurs provides valuable insights into the Earth's past, evolution, and the diversity of life that once inhabited our planet.

Fossil discoveries and paleontology

Fossil discoveries and paleontology play a crucial role in our understanding of prehistoric life, including dinosaurs. Here's an overview of their significance:

1. **Preservation:** Fossils are the remains or traces of ancient organisms that have been preserved in rock over millions of years. They provide direct evidence of past life forms, allowing scientists to study their anatomy, behaviors, and ecological roles.

2. **Dinosaur Reconstruction:** Fossils allow paleontologists to reconstruct the appearance, size, and features of dinosaurs. By studying bones, teeth, and other remains, researchers can create detailed models and illustrations of how these creatures looked and lived.

3. **Evolutionary Insights:** Fossils help scientists understand the evolutionary history of dinosaurs and their relationships to other organisms. By comparing fossil evidence, researchers can trace the development of various dinosaur groups and their ancestors.

4. **Behavior and Ecology:** Fossilized footprints, nests, and eggs provide insights into the behaviors and reproductive strategies of dinosaurs. These traces offer valuable information about their interactions, movements, and nesting habits.

5. **Environmental Context:** Fossil sites also reveal details about the ancient environments in which dinosaurs lived. By studying the sediment and plant remains found alongside fossils, researchers can reconstruct

the ecosystems and climates of the past.

6. **Extinction Events:** The most famous mass extinction event that led to the demise of non-avian dinosaurs occurred around 66 million years ago. Fossil evidence helps scientists understand the causes and effects of these events on Earth's biodiversity.

7. **Technological Advances:** Advancements in technology, such as computed tomography (CT) scanning and 3D modeling, allow researchers to study fossils without damaging them. This enables detailed examination of internal structures and even DNA analysis in some cases.

8. **Education and Outreach:** Fossil discoveries capture the public's imagination and inspire interest in science. Museums and educational institutions use fossils to engage people of all ages in learning about Earth's history and the diversity of life that existed long before humans.

9. **Ongoing Research:** Paleontology is an active field, and new discoveries are made regularly. Fossils shed light on previously unknown species, behaviors, and ecosystems, constantly expanding our knowledge of the ancient world.

10. **Conservation:** Studying fossils can provide insights into the effects of environmental changes and extinction events. This knowledge can inform modern conservation efforts and help us understand the potential impacts of climate change on current species.

Overall, fossil discoveries and paleontology provide a window into the past, offering glimpses of worlds that existed long before our time. Through careful excavation, analysis, and research, scientists continue to unlock the mysteries of ancient life and the incredible diversity of creatures that once roamed the Earth, including the iconic dinosaurs.

Theories about their extinction

The extinction of the non-avian dinosaurs at the end of the Cretaceous period, around 66 million years ago, is one of the most well-known and debated events in Earth's history. Several theories have been proposed to explain their extinction, and it's likely that a combination of factors played a role. Here are some of the leading theories:

1. **Asteroid Impact (Impact Hypothesis):** One of the most widely accepted theories is that a massive asteroid or comet impact caused a catastrophic event known as the Chicxulub impact. This impact, which occurred in what is now the Yucatan Peninsula of Mexico, would have released an immense amount of energy, causing massive wildfires, tsunamis, and a "nuclear winter" effect. The resulting environmental disruptions, including the blocking of sunlight and a dramatic drop in temperatures, would have severely impacted ecosystems, leading to a collapse of food chains and the extinction of many species, including the non-avian dinosaurs.

2. **Volcanic Activity (Volcanism Hypothesis):** Another prominent theory suggests that massive volcanic activity, specifically the eruption of the Deccan Traps in present-day India, contributed to the extinction event. These volcanic eruptions would have released large amounts of gases and particles into the atmosphere, causing climate disruptions, acid rain, and a cooling effect. The resulting environmental stress could have led to widespread extinction by

affecting food sources and habitats.

3. **Climate Change:** Natural climate fluctuations could have played a role in the dinosaurs' decline. Over long time scales, Earth's climate naturally changes due to factors such as variations in the Earth's orbit, solar radiation, and volcanic activity. Gradual climate shifts could have led to changes in ecosystems, altering the availability of food and habitats for dinosaurs.

4. **Disease:** Some researchers have proposed that disease outbreaks could have contributed to the extinction event. Rapid spread of diseases could have affected both plant and animal populations, disrupting ecosystems and leading to extinctions.

5. **Combination of Factors:** Many scientists believe that a combination of several factors, including the impact event, volcanic activity, and climate change, worked together to create a "perfect storm" of environmental disruption. This scenario would have amplified the stress on ecosystems, leading to a cascading effect that resulted in mass extinctions.

It's important to note that these theories are not mutually exclusive, and it's likely that a combination of factors contributed to the extinction event. The discovery of the Chicxulub impact crater and evidence of Deccan Traps volcanism provide support for the asteroid impact and volcanism hypotheses. However, ongoing research and new discoveries continue to refine our understanding of this pivotal event in Earth's history and the role it played in shaping the evolution of life on our planet.

Canidae: Dogs & Wolves

Canidae is the biological family that includes a diverse group of carnivorous mammals known as canids. This family includes a wide range of species, from domestic dogs to wolves, foxes, jackals, and other closely related animals. Dogs (Canis lupus familiaris) and wolves (Canis lupus) are two of the most well-known members of the Canidae family.

Dogs (Canis lupus familiaris): Domestic dogs are descendants of wolves and have been selectively bred by humans for various purposes, resulting in a wide variety of breeds with different sizes, shapes, and temperaments. Dogs have been our companions and working partners for thousands of years, fulfilling roles such as hunting, herding, guarding, and providing emotional support. Their close relationship with humans has led to a wide range of behaviors and adaptations, and they exhibit a remarkable ability to understand human cues and communicate with us.

Wolves (Canis lupus): Wolves are highly social and intelligent animals that have played a significant role in various ecosystems as apex predators. They live and hunt in family units called packs, which are usually led by an alpha pair. Wolves are known for their complex communication through vocalizations, body language, and facial expressions. They are skilled hunters, preying on a variety of large and small animals. Despite their predatory nature, wolves also play a crucial role in maintaining the health and balance of ecosystems by controlling prey populations and influencing vegetation.

Conservation and Coexistence: Wolves and dogs share a

common ancestor and have a high degree of genetic similarity. The conservation of wolves is important for maintaining biodiversity and healthy ecosystems. However, conflicts can arise between wolves and humans, particularly in areas where livestock is present. Efforts to manage these conflicts while preserving wolf populations involve implementing non-lethal methods of predator deterrents, habitat conservation, and public education.

The relationship between dogs and humans is a unique and enduring example of interspecies cooperation and companionship. Dogs have become an integral part of human society, serving roles as companions, working animals, service animals, and therapy animals. Studying the behavior and biology of canids, including dogs and wolves, not only enhances our understanding of their evolutionary history but also provides insights into animal cognition, social behavior, and the ways in which animals and humans coexist.

Domestication of dogs and their roles

The domestication of dogs (Canis lupus familiaris) is one of the most remarkable examples of human-animal interaction and partnership. The process of domestication involves the gradual adaptation of wild animals to living alongside humans and fulfilling specific roles that benefit both species. Dogs are believed to be one of the first animals domesticated by humans, and their unique bond with humans has had a profound impact on both species' evolution and development.

Key Points in the Domestication of Dogs:

1. **Origins:** The exact timeline and location of dog domestication are still debated, but evidence suggests that it began tens of thousands of years ago in different regions around the world. Dogs are descendants of wolves, with the domestication process likely involving mutual benefits for both humans and wolves.

2. **Mutual Benefits:** Early humans likely encountered wolves scavenging around human campsites, leading to a mutually beneficial relationship. Wolves that were less aggressive and more sociable may have gained access to human food sources, while humans benefited from wolves' hunting skills, protection, and alertness to danger.

3. **Behavioral Changes:** Over generations, the wolves that displayed less fear and aggression toward humans were more likely to thrive in the human environment. These behavioral traits were passed down to their offspring, resulting in a gradual shift from wild

wolves to a more cooperative and sociable species that eventually became dogs.

Roles of Domestic Dogs:

1. **Companionship:** One of the primary roles of domestic dogs is to provide companionship and emotional support to humans. Dogs have evolved to be highly attuned to human emotions and behaviors, making them excellent companions for people of all ages.

2. **Working Partners:** Dogs have been bred and trained to perform various tasks, including herding livestock, guarding property, pulling sleds, and assisting people with disabilities. Service dogs are trained to perform specific tasks that aid individuals with mobility, sensory, or medical challenges.

3. **Search and Rescue:** Dogs have exceptional olfactory senses, which make them valuable in search and rescue operations. They can locate missing persons, detect drugs or explosives, and assist in disaster relief efforts.

4. **Therapy Animals:** Dogs are often used as therapy animals in healthcare settings to provide comfort, reduce stress, and improve the emotional well-being of patients. Their presence can have positive effects on individuals in hospitals, nursing homes, and rehabilitation centers.

5. **Recreation:** Dogs provide opportunities for recreational activities such as walking, running, playing, and training. These activities promote physical exercise, mental stimulation, and social interaction for both dogs and humans.

6. **Scientific Research:** Dogs are also valuable subjects in scientific research, contributing to studies on behavior, genetics, health, and cognition. Their close relationship with humans allows researchers to gain

insights into a wide range of topics.

The domestication of dogs has had a profound impact on human society and culture. Dogs have become integral members of households and communities, enriching our lives with their loyalty, companionship, and diverse abilities. As we continue to learn about the genetics, behavior, and evolution of domestic dogs, we gain a deeper understanding of the intricate relationship between humans and animals.

Wolves' social structures and pack dynamics

Wolves (Canis lupus) are highly social animals that live and hunt in cooperative family groups known as packs. Their social structures and pack dynamics are complex and play a crucial role in their survival and reproduction. Here's an overview of wolves' social structures and pack dynamics:

Pack Structure:

1. **Family Units:** A wolf pack typically consists of a family unit composed of a breeding pair, known as the alpha or dominant male and female, and their offspring from one or more breeding seasons. These offspring are known as pups or subordinates.
2. **Hierarchical Order:** Within a pack, there is a hierarchical order based on dominance and submission. The alpha pair holds the highest rank, followed by beta wolves (subordinates), and lower-ranking wolves. Dominance is established through displays of aggression, body language, and vocalizations.

Pack Dynamics:

1. **Cooperative Hunting:** One of the primary advantages of wolf pack dynamics is cooperative hunting. Wolves work together to pursue and bring down prey animals that are often larger than an individual wolf could handle. Pack members use strategies like encircling, chasing, and cornering to capture prey.
2. **Territorial Behavior:** Wolf packs defend a territory

that includes their den site, hunting grounds, and resources. Territories can range from several square miles to over a hundred square miles, depending on prey availability. Packs mark their territory with scent markings and vocalizations.

3. **Reproduction and Rearing Pups:** Breeding occurs within the alpha pair, which is usually the only pair to produce offspring in the pack. Other pack members help care for and protect the pups, bringing them food and assisting in their socialization and training.

4. **Communication:** Wolves use complex vocalizations, body postures, and facial expressions to communicate with pack members. Howling is an important form of long-distance communication, allowing wolves to communicate their presence, location, and readiness for activities.

5. **Dispersal:** As young wolves mature, they may disperse from their natal pack to find new territories and potentially form new packs. This dispersal helps prevent inbreeding and maintains genetic diversity.

6. **Social Bonding:** Wolves' social behaviors are important for maintaining social bonds within the pack. Playful behaviors among pack members, such as wrestling and chasing, help strengthen these bonds and contribute to the overall cohesion of the group.

7. **Leadership:** While the alpha pair often takes the lead in decision-making, the pack's direction is also influenced by the behaviors and interactions of other pack members. Cooperation and coordination are essential for successful hunting and survival.

Wolves' social structures and pack dynamics are adaptations that have evolved over time to increase their chances of survival and successful reproduction. While there can be variations in pack size, structure, and behaviors based on environmental conditions and prey availability, the cooperative nature of wolf packs remains a remarkable example of social behavior in the animal kingdom.

Relationship between humans and dogs

The relationship between humans and dogs is one of the most ancient and unique partnerships in the animal kingdom. This bond has evolved over thousands of years and is characterized by mutual companionship, cooperation, and emotional attachment. Here are some key aspects of the relationship between humans and dogs:

1. **Domestication:** Dogs are believed to have been domesticated from wolves tens of thousands of years ago. This process marked the beginning of a mutually beneficial relationship, with dogs providing assistance to humans in various tasks while receiving food, protection, and companionship in return.

2. **Companionship:** Dogs are known for their loyalty, affection, and ability to form strong emotional bonds with their human companions. They provide companionship, comfort, and a sense of purpose to people of all ages, from children to the elderly.

3. **Working Partners:** Throughout history, dogs have served as working partners for humans in various roles, including hunting, herding, guarding, and even assisting people with disabilities. Working dog breeds have been bred and trained to excel in specific tasks, showcasing their intelligence, trainability, and willingness to cooperate with humans.

4. **Therapy and Assistance:** Dogs are often used as therapy animals to provide emotional support and comfort to individuals in hospitals, nursing homes, and rehabilitation centers. Service dogs are trained to

assist people with disabilities, performing tasks such as guiding the visually impaired, alerting the hearing impaired, and helping individuals with mobility challenges.

5. **Emotional Support:** Dogs have been shown to have a positive impact on human mental health, reducing stress, anxiety, and loneliness. The act of petting a dog can release oxytocin, a hormone associated with bonding and positive emotions.

6. **Communication:** Dogs are highly attuned to human cues and body language, making them adept at understanding and responding to human communication. They can learn commands, recognize their owners' voices, and respond to non-verbal signals.

7. **Social Behavior:** Dogs exhibit social behaviors that are similar to those of humans and other social mammals. They form hierarchies within packs, and when integrated into human families, they often see their human owners as their pack leaders.

8. **Evolution of Breeds:** Humans have selectively bred dogs for various traits, resulting in the diverse array of dog breeds we see today. Each breed has unique characteristics, behaviors, and appearances that make them suitable for specific roles and lifestyles.

9. **Cultural Significance:** Dogs have left a lasting impact on human culture, appearing in folklore, literature, art, and religious symbolism. They are often portrayed as loyal and faithful companions, exemplifying qualities that humans admire.

10. **Responsible Ownership:** The relationship between humans and dogs also comes with responsibilities. Responsible pet ownership includes providing proper care, training, and healthcare for dogs to ensure their well-being.

The relationship between humans and dogs is a testament to the deep emotional and practical connections that can develop between different species. It showcases the potential for cooperation, understanding, and affection that can exist between humans and animals, enriching the lives of both parties involved.

Chondrichthyes: Fish & Sharks

Chondrichthyes, commonly known as cartilaginous fish, include two well-known groups: sharks and rays. These ancient creatures have evolved unique adaptations that have allowed them to thrive in a variety of aquatic environments. Here are some key aspects of Chondrichthyes, including fish and sharks:

1. **Cartilaginous Skeleton:** One of the defining features of Chondrichthyes is their cartilaginous skeleton, which is made of flexible cartilage rather than bone. This characteristic gives them a lightweight and flexible body structure.

2. **Marine Habitat:** Most Chondrichthyes species are found in marine environments, ranging from shallow coastal waters to deep ocean regions. Sharks, in particular, are known for their ability to inhabit diverse marine habitats, from coral reefs to open ocean.

3. **Predatory Adaptations:** Many shark species are apex predators, occupying the top of the marine food chain. They have evolved a range of adaptations for hunting and capturing prey, including sharp teeth, powerful jaws, and excellent senses of smell and electroreception.

4. **Diverse Species:** Chondrichthyes exhibit a wide variety of species with diverse sizes, shapes, and behaviors. Sharks come in various sizes, from the enormous filter-feeding whale shark to the small and elusive lanternsharks.

5. **Shark Reproduction:** Sharks have diverse reproductive

strategies. Some species give birth to live young (viviparity), while others lay eggs (oviparity) or retain the eggs inside the body until they hatch (ovoviviparity).

6. **Importance to Ecosystems:** Chondrichthyes play a crucial role in marine ecosystems as top predators, helping to regulate the populations of other marine species. They also contribute to maintaining the balance of ocean food webs.

7. **Threats and Conservation:** Many species of Chondrichthyes are currently facing threats due to overfishing, habitat destruction, and accidental bycatch. Conservation efforts are important to ensure the survival of these ancient and ecologically important creatures.

8. **Rays and Skates:** Rays and skates are closely related to sharks and are part of the Chondrichthyes group. They have flattened bodies and unique adaptations for life on the ocean floor. Some rays have specialized adaptations, such as electric organs for hunting and communication.

9. **Shark Behavior:** Sharks exhibit a wide range of behaviors, from solitary to social. Some species are migratory and travel long distances in search of food or suitable breeding grounds.

10. **Public Perception:** Sharks have captured the public's imagination as powerful and mysterious creatures. However, negative portrayals of sharks in media have led to misconceptions and unjust fear of these animals.

11. **Ecotourism and Education:** In recent years, shark ecotourism has gained popularity as a way to educate the public about the importance of sharks and promote their conservation. Observing sharks in their natural habitat helps dispel myths and foster appreciation for these animals.

12. **Shark Research:** Scientists study sharks to better understand their behavior, biology, and ecological role. Research efforts help inform conservation strategies and support the sustainable management of shark populations.

The world of Chondrichthyes, including fish and sharks, is a fascinating one that offers insights into the diversity of life in aquatic environments and the intricate balance of marine ecosystems. Their unique adaptations, behaviors, and ecological significance make them subjects of ongoing scientific exploration and conservation efforts.

Diversity of fish species and habitats

Fish are incredibly diverse creatures that inhabit a wide range of aquatic habitats, from freshwater rivers and lakes to the vast oceans. Their adaptability to various environments has led to the evolution of numerous species, each with unique characteristics suited to their specific habitats. Here's an overview of the diversity of fish species and their habitats:

1. **Freshwater Fish:**
   - **Rivers and Streams:** Many species of fish thrive in flowing freshwater habitats, where they can navigate the currents and find shelter among rocks and vegetation. Examples include trout, salmon, and catfish.
   - **Lakes and Ponds:** Lakes and ponds provide still water habitats for fish like bass, perch, and sunfish. These environments can vary in size and depth, influencing the types of species that inhabit them.
   - **Swamps and Marshes:** Some fish are adapted to the shallow and often murky waters of swamps and marshes. These habitats support species such as mudfish and killifish.
2. **Marine Fish:**
   - **Coral Reefs:** Coral reefs are home to a diverse array of fish species that rely on the complex structures of coral formations for shelter and protection. Examples include clownfish, parrotfish, and angelfish.
   - **Open Ocean:** The vast open ocean is inhabited

by pelagic fish that swim in the water column. These include tuna, swordfish, and mahi-mahi, which are adapted for life in the open water.

- **Deep Sea:** The deep sea is inhabited by a unique range of fish species adapted to survive in extreme pressures and darkness. Deep-sea anglerfish and gulper eels are examples of these mysterious creatures.

3. **Estuaries and Mangroves:**

- **Estuaries:** Estuaries, where freshwater meets the sea, are vital nurseries for many fish species. Young fish find protection in these nutrient-rich areas. Examples include flounder, mullet, and snook.
- **Mangroves:** Mangrove forests provide shelter and breeding grounds for various fish species. Their intricate root systems offer protection for juvenile fish and other aquatic organisms.

4. **Arctic and Antarctic Waters:**

- **Polar Fish:** In the cold waters of the Arctic and Antarctic, fish such as Arctic cod and Antarctic toothfish have evolved to survive in extreme cold temperatures and icy conditions.

5. **Freshwater and Marine Transitions:**

- **Diadromous Fish:** Some fish species, like salmon, eels, and sturgeon, migrate between freshwater and marine environments for various stages of their life cycle. This migration is known as diadromy.

6. **Cave Fish:**

- **Subterranean Habitats:** Fish living in underground caves have adapted to life in darkness and often have unique features, such as reduced eyesight or heightened sensory adaptations.

7. **Endangered Habitats:**

- **Coral Reefs and Mangroves:** Coral reefs and mangroves are critically endangered due to human activities such as pollution, overfishing, and climate change. Protecting these habitats is essential for the survival of many fish species.

The incredible diversity of fish species and their habitats reflects the intricate interplay between aquatic ecosystems and the adaptations that fish have developed over millions of years. Understanding and conserving these habitats is vital for maintaining the health of our oceans, freshwater systems, and the countless species that depend on them.

Unique features of sharks and their role in marine ecosystems

Sharks are fascinating creatures with unique features that make them well-suited for life in marine ecosystems. Their role in these ecosystems is essential for maintaining balance and health. Here are some of the unique features of sharks and their important role in marine ecosystems:

1. Apex Predators: Sharks are top predators in many marine food chains, regulating the populations of their prey species and preventing them from becoming overly abundant. This helps maintain the overall health and balance of the ecosystem.

2. Adaptations for Swimming: Sharks have streamlined bodies and powerful muscles that enable them to swim efficiently and with speed. Their unique shape reduces drag, allowing them to move through the water with minimal resistance.

3. Cartilaginous Skeleton: Unlike most fish, sharks have a cartilaginous skeleton instead of bones. This lightweight and flexible structure gives them an advantage in buoyancy and allows for faster movements.

4. Powerful Senses: Sharks have highly developed senses, including acute vision, excellent sense of smell, and sensitive electroreceptors. These senses help them locate prey, navigate their environment, and detect changes in water pressure and electrical fields.

5. Apex Predator Regulation: As apex predators, sharks help control the populations of lower-level predators and herbivores.

This prevents the overgrazing of marine vegetation and ensures the survival of important species in the food chain.

6. Cleaning Ecosystems: Some shark species, like the nurse shark, play a role in cleaning marine ecosystems by feeding on dead or injured animals. This helps prevent the spread of diseases and keeps the environment clean.

7. Indicator Species: The presence and health of shark populations can serve as indicators of the overall health of marine ecosystems. Declines in shark populations can signal overfishing or ecosystem imbalances.

8. Ecotourism and Education: Sharks contribute to ecotourism by attracting divers and snorkelers who want to observe these majestic creatures in their natural habitat. This can generate income for local economies and raise awareness about marine conservation.

9. Nutrient Cycling: When sharks consume prey, they help transfer nutrients between different parts of the marine ecosystem. This contributes to nutrient cycling and maintains the health of marine habitats.

10. Biodiversity: The various shark species contribute to the overall biodiversity of marine ecosystems. Each species has a unique ecological role, enhancing the complexity and resilience of these systems.

Despite their crucial role in marine ecosystems, many shark species are facing threats such as overfishing, habitat destruction, and bycatch. Conservation efforts are essential to protect these apex predators and maintain the health of marine ecosystems. Understanding and appreciating the unique features and importance of sharks can inspire efforts to ensure their survival and the preservation of the oceans they inhabit.

Shark conservation and protection

Shark conservation and protection are essential to maintain the health and balance of marine ecosystems and ensure the survival of these iconic apex predators. Sharks face various threats due to human activities, including overfishing, bycatch, habitat degradation, and climate change. Here are some strategies and initiatives for shark conservation and protection:

1. Fishing Regulations: Implementing and enforcing fishing regulations is crucial to prevent overfishing of shark populations. These regulations can include size limits, catch quotas, and fishing bans in critical habitats and during vulnerable times, such as during breeding seasons.

2. Shark Sanctuaries: Establishing protected areas, or shark sanctuaries, where fishing and other human activities are restricted or prohibited, can provide safe havens for shark populations to thrive and reproduce.

3. Sustainable Fishing Practices: Encouraging sustainable fishing practices, such as using circle hooks and other shark-friendly gear, can reduce the unintentional capture of sharks as bycatch.

4. Endangered Species Protections: Listing endangered shark species under national and international conservation agreements, such as the Convention on International Trade in Endangered Species of Wild Fauna and Flora (CITES), can provide legal protections and regulate international trade.

5. International Collaboration: Collaborative efforts between countries, organizations, and stakeholders are essential for effective shark conservation. Sharing data, research findings, and best practices can lead to more informed decision-making.

6. Awareness and Education: Raising public awareness about the importance of sharks and the threats they face can foster a sense of responsibility and support for conservation efforts. Education programs and campaigns can dispel myths and promote positive attitudes toward sharks.

7. Research and Monitoring: Conducting scientific research on shark populations, migration patterns, and behavior helps inform conservation strategies. Long-term monitoring can track population trends and assess the effectiveness of conservation measures.

8. Ecotourism and Sustainable Livelihoods: Promoting shark ecotourism can provide economic incentives for communities to protect sharks and their habitats. Sustainable livelihoods, such as diving tours to observe sharks in their natural habitat, can offer alternatives to destructive fishing practices.

9. Collaboration with Fishers: Engaging with local fishing communities to develop and implement shark-friendly practices can reduce conflicts and encourage sustainable resource use.

10. Technology and Innovation: Utilizing technology such as satellite tracking, underwater cameras, and genetic analysis can improve our understanding of shark behavior, migration, and population dynamics.

11. Policy Advocacy: Advocacy for strong conservation policies at local, national, and international levels can lead to legal protections and increased funding for shark conservation initiatives.

Shark conservation is a global effort that requires collaboration across borders and disciplines. By addressing the threats to shark populations and implementing effective conservation strategies, we can ensure the survival of these remarkable creatures and contribute to the health and resilience of marine ecosystems.

Equidae: Horses

Equidae is a family of mammals that includes horses, donkeys, and zebras. These animals are known for their unique evolutionary history, remarkable adaptations, and important roles in human history. Here are some key aspects of Equidae, specifically focusing on horses:

1. Evolution and Taxonomy: Equidae belongs to the order Perissodactyla, which includes odd-toed ungulates. Horses, donkeys, and zebras are closely related and share a common evolutionary ancestry.

2. Anatomy and Adaptations: Horses are well-adapted for a life of running and grazing. They have long legs with a single toe, strong muscles, and a streamlined body shape that allows them to achieve high speeds. Their teeth have evolved for efficient grinding of plant material.

3. Domestication: Horses were domesticated by humans thousands of years ago and played a significant role in agriculture, transportation, warfare, and cultural activities. They facilitated trade, exploration, and communication between different civilizations.

4. Breeds and Uses: There are numerous horse breeds that have been selectively bred for various purposes, such as racing, agriculture, riding, and show. Some breeds are known for their speed, while others are prized for their strength and endurance.

5. Behavior and Communication: Horses are social animals that live in groups known as herds. They communicate through body language, vocalizations, and facial expressions. Understanding horse behavior is important for their proper care and training.

6. Equine Care and Health: Proper care of horses includes providing them with a balanced diet, shelter, exercise, and regular veterinary care. Horses can suffer from various health issues, including lameness, colic, and dental problems.

7. Equine Sports and Recreation: Horses are involved in various sports and recreational activities, such as horse racing, show jumping, dressage, rodeo events, and trail riding. These activities require specialized training and skills.

8. Conservation and Welfare: The conservation of wild equids, such as zebras and wild asses, is important to maintain genetic diversity and preserve these species in their natural habitats. Additionally, animal welfare organizations work to ensure the well-being of domestic horses and prevent neglect or abuse.

9. Equine-Assisted Therapy: Horses are also used in therapeutic interventions for individuals with physical, cognitive, or emotional challenges. Equine-assisted therapy can help improve self-esteem, communication, and overall well-being.

10. Research and Education: Research on equine genetics, behavior, nutrition, and health contributes to our understanding of these animals and informs best practices for their care and management.

Horses have been an integral part of human history, culture, and development. Whether serving as transportation, companions, or participants in sports and therapy, horses continue to enrich our lives in various ways. Understanding their biology, behavior, and interactions with humans is crucial for their proper care, conservation, and coexistence.

Evolution and domestication of horses

Evolution of Horses: The evolutionary history of horses spans millions of years, beginning with small, multi-toed ancestors and culminating in the single-toed, large equines we are familiar with today. Here are the key stages in the evolution of horses:

1. Eocene Epoch: About 56 million years ago, the first known ancestor of horses, known as Eohippus or Hyracotherium, appeared. These animals were small, forest-dwelling creatures with several toes on each foot.

2. Miocene Epoch: Over time, horses underwent significant changes in body size, teeth structure, and limb adaptations. They gradually evolved from browsing on soft vegetation to grazing on tougher grasses. The middle Miocene saw the emergence of genera like Merychippus and Pliohippus.

3. Pliocene Epoch: By the late Pliocene, about 3 million years ago, the modern Equus lineage had emerged. These horses had a single toe on each foot, specialized teeth for grazing, and adaptations for running on open grasslands.

Domestication of Horses: Horses were domesticated by humans around 4000-3500 BCE, marking a pivotal moment in human history. The domestication process took place independently in different regions, resulting in various horse breeds adapted to specific tasks and environments. Here's an overview of horse domestication:

1. Role of Wild Horses: Initially, humans likely interacted with wild horse populations, observing their behavior and habits. As humans transitioned from hunting-gathering to agriculture, they recognized the potential of harnessing horses for tasks such as transportation, plowing, and carrying goods.

2. Domestication Centers: Horse domestication occurred in different regions around the world. The Botai culture in Kazakhstan is one of the earliest known sites of horse domestication, around 3500 BCE. Other regions, like the Eurasian steppes, the Middle East, and China, also played significant roles.

3. Selective Breeding: Over generations, humans selectively bred horses for specific traits, such as strength, speed, endurance, and temperament. Different breeds emerged to fulfill various roles, such as workhorses, warhorses, and riding horses.

4. Societal Impact: The domestication of horses had a profound impact on human societies. It revolutionized transportation, allowing for faster travel and the establishment of trade routes. Horses were essential for agriculture, warfare, exploration, and cultural practices.

5. Evolution of Breeds: As domestication progressed, distinct breeds emerged through intentional breeding practices. Breeds like the Arabian horse, known for its endurance, and the Andalusian horse, prized for its elegance, showcase the diverse roles that horses played in human societies.

6. Modern Horse Breeding: Today, horse breeding continues with a focus on refining specific traits for various purposes, such as racing, sport, work, and companionship. Breed registries and organizations ensure the preservation of breed standards and genetic diversity.

Horse evolution and domestication are remarkable stories of coevolution between humans and animals. The partnership between humans and horses has shaped cultures, economies, and civilizations throughout history. Understanding the evolutionary journey of horses and their domestication enhances our appreciation for their contributions to our world.

Various horse breeds and their uses

Horse breeds have been developed over centuries to serve specific purposes, whether it's in agriculture, transportation, sports, or companionship. Here are some notable horse breeds and their primary uses:

1. **Arabian:** Known for their distinctive head shape and high tail carriage, Arabian horses are prized for their endurance, intelligence, and loyalty. They excel in endurance riding and are also used in various equestrian disciplines.

2. **Thoroughbred:** Thoroughbreds are renowned for their speed and agility, making them the stars of horse racing. Their sleek build and competitive nature make them a favorite in the racing world.

3. **Quarter Horse:** A versatile breed known for their strength and athleticism, Quarter Horses are often used in rodeos, Western riding, and ranch work. They excel in short-distance races and agility events.

4. **Andalusian:** Known for their elegance and beauty, Andalusian horses are often used in dressage, as well as various forms of classical and high-level riding. Their strong build and graceful movements make them sought after in the show ring.

5. **Clydesdale:** Clydesdales are large draft horses known for their strength and distinctive feathered legs. They were historically used for heavy farm work and pulling wagons, but today they are often seen in parades and promotional events.

6. **Belgian:** Another powerful draft breed, Belgian horses are known for their gentle temperament and strength. They were

traditionally used for heavy agricultural work and logging.

7. Appaloosa: Appaloosas are recognized for their unique coat patterns and versatile nature. They are used in a variety of equestrian disciplines, including trail riding, Western riding, and even dressage.

8. Paint: Paint horses have a distinctive coat pattern characterized by large patches of white and other colors. They are used in a range of activities, including Western riding, trail riding, and pleasure riding.

9. Hanoverian: Hanoverians are a popular breed in dressage and jumping competitions. They are known for their athleticism, trainability, and elegant appearance.

10. Friesian: Friesians are known for their striking black coat, long mane, and tail. They are often used in driving, dressage, and exhibitions due to their beauty and presence.

11. Morgan: Morgan horses are known for their versatility and strong work ethic. They excel in a wide range of disciplines, including driving, dressage, trail riding, and ranch work.

12. Mustang: Mustangs are wild horses that have been descendants of Spanish horses and other breeds. They are often captured and trained for various purposes, including trail riding and competitions.

13. Shetland Pony: Shetland ponies are small, hardy, and versatile. They were historically used for working in coal mines and are now popular as children's ponies and in driving competitions.

14. Icelandic Horse: Icelandic horses are known for their unique gaits and hardiness. They are used for riding, driving, and often participate in traditional gaited competitions.

These are just a few examples of the diverse horse breeds and their respective uses. Each breed's unique characteristics make them well-suited to specific tasks, and their roles continue to evolve with changing societal needs and equestrian disciplines.

Equine-assisted therapy and equestrian sports

Equine-assisted therapy and equestrian sports are two important aspects of the relationship between humans and horses. They both involve interactions with horses, but they serve different purposes and have distinct benefits.

Equine-Assisted Therapy: Equine-assisted therapy, also known as equine-assisted psychotherapy or horse therapy, involves using interactions with horses to address various physical, emotional, and mental health issues in individuals. This type of therapy is often conducted by trained professionals, such as therapists, psychologists, or counselors, who work alongside horses to facilitate therapeutic experiences. Some key points about equine-assisted therapy include:

1. **Emotional and Psychological Benefits:** Horses are known for their sensitivity to human emotions and can mirror clients' feelings. Working with horses can help individuals develop self-awareness, emotional regulation, empathy, and improved communication skills.

2. **Physical Benefits:** Equine-assisted therapy can also provide physical benefits, such as improved coordination, balance, and muscle strength. Activities like grooming, riding, and leading horses can enhance physical well-being.

3. **Confidence and Self-Esteem:** Achieving goals and building relationships with horses can boost self-confidence and self-esteem. Overcoming challenges in the presence of a supportive horse can lead to personal growth.

4. **Trust and Bonding:** Establishing a connection with a horse requires trust and effective communication. Developing a bond with a horse can translate to improved interpersonal relationships outside of therapy.

5. **Populations Served:** Equine-assisted therapy can benefit individuals of all ages and backgrounds, including children with developmental challenges, individuals with PTSD, people dealing with anxiety or depression, and those in addiction recovery.

Equestrian Sports: Equestrian sports encompass a wide range of competitive activities that involve riding and working with horses. These sports require skill, technique, and a strong partnership between horse and rider. Some popular equestrian sports include:

1. **Dressage:** A disciplined sport that involves precision and harmony between horse and rider. Dressage focuses on executing precise movements and patterns.

2. **Show Jumping:** Competitors navigate a series of jumps in an arena, aiming to complete the course without knocking down any obstacles or exceeding the time limit.

3. **Eventing:** Also known as the "equestrian triathlon," eventing combines dressage, cross-country jumping, and show jumping.

4. **Western Riding:** A style rooted in traditional ranch work, western riding includes rodeo events, reining, and other activities that showcase practical horsemanship.

5. **Endurance Riding:** Involves long-distance races that test the horse and rider's stamina and teamwork over challenging terrain.

6. **Polo:** Players on horseback use mallets to hit a ball into the opposing team's goal, requiring both riding skill

and strategic play.

7. **Rodeo Events:** Rodeo includes activities such as bull riding, barrel racing, and roping, showcasing skills used in working with livestock.
8. **Vaulting:** A gymnastic sport performed on the back of a moving horse, combining athleticism and horsemanship.

Both equine-assisted therapy and equestrian sports showcase the unique and multifaceted relationship between humans and horses. While equine-assisted therapy focuses on the therapeutic benefits of working with horses, equestrian sports celebrate the physical skill, teamwork, and mutual respect between horse and rider in competitive settings.

Insecta & Arachnida: Insects & Spiders

Insecta & Arachnida: Exploring Insects & Spiders

Insects and spiders, belonging to the classes Insecta and Arachnida respectively, constitute a diverse and abundant group of arthropods that play crucial roles in ecosystems and impact human life in various ways. From their incredible diversity to their essential ecological functions, these tiny creatures have captured the curiosity of scientists, enthusiasts, and nature lovers alike.

Introduction to Insects & Spiders: Insects and spiders are arthropods, characterized by their jointed legs and segmented bodies. They inhabit almost every habitat on Earth, from the depths of the ocean to high mountain peaks. With millions of known species and likely many more yet to be discovered, insects and spiders are integral to the web of life on our planet.

Biodiversity and Adaptations: The diversity within the insect and spider world is astounding. Insects encompass a vast range of forms, from delicate butterflies to resilient beetles. Similarly, spiders exhibit a wide variety of adaptations, from the intricate web-spinning capabilities of orb-weavers to the stealthy hunting strategies of wolf spiders.

Ecological Significance: Insects and spiders play critical roles in ecosystems as pollinators, decomposers, and predators. Pollinators like bees and butterflies facilitate the reproduction of flowering plants, ensuring the production of fruits and seeds.

Decomposers, such as dung beetles, recycle organic matter, enriching soil fertility. Meanwhile, predatory spiders help control insect populations, maintaining a balance in the food chain.

Human Impact and Benefits: Insects and spiders profoundly influence human life. Bees pollinate many of the crops that contribute to our diets, while silkworms provide the fibers for textiles. However, some insects are pests that damage crops and spread diseases. Understanding their behavior and biology is crucial for sustainable agriculture and disease prevention.

Insect Behavior and Communication: Insects exhibit a wide array of behaviors, from the coordinated dances of honeybees to the metamorphic transformations of butterflies. Communication among insects often involves chemical cues, sounds, vibrations, and visual displays, which enable them to mate, forage, and defend territories.

Spider Silk and Webs: Spiders are renowned for their silk-producing abilities, which they use to spin intricate webs for trapping prey and creating shelters. Spider silk is incredibly strong and flexible, with applications in fields ranging from materials science to medical research.

Conservation and Threats: While insects and spiders are essential to ecosystems, many species are facing threats from habitat loss, pollution, and climate change. The decline in pollinators, such as bees, has raised concerns about the sustainability of agricultural systems and food production.

Education and Appreciation: Studying insects and spiders provides valuable insights into the natural world and the complex interactions that shape ecosystems. Engaging with these creatures fosters a deeper appreciation for their beauty, diversity, and ecological importance.

Exploring Insects & Spiders: This comprehensive guide delves into the captivating world of insects and spiders, from their astonishing diversity and behaviors to their vital roles in sustaining life on Earth. Join us on a journey to discover the intricate lives of these small but mighty creatures that have been weaving their way through the fabric of our planet for millions of years.

Overview of insect and spider diversity

Insect and Spider Diversity: A World of Wonders

The world of insects and spiders is a realm of unparalleled diversity and fascination. With millions of species identified and countless more awaiting discovery, these arthropods span an astonishing array of forms, behaviors, and ecological roles. From the smallest ants to the largest tarantulas, insects and spiders have evolved to occupy virtually every corner of our planet, from the depths of oceans to the heights of mountain ranges.

Insect Diversity: Insects belong to the class Insecta, and they are the most diverse group of animals on Earth. With over a million known species and estimates suggesting there could be several million more yet to be discovered, insects come in an incredible range of shapes, sizes, colors, and adaptations. They can be found in nearly every habitat, from tropical rainforests to deserts, and even inside our homes.

Spider Diversity: Spiders, part of the class Arachnida, also boast a remarkable diversity. While they are not insects (spiders are arachnids), they are equally intriguing in their own right. There are thousands of recognized spider species, each exhibiting unique behaviors and attributes. Spiders can be found in environments as diverse as forests, grasslands, and urban areas, often lurking in hidden corners or crafting intricate webs.

Morphological Adaptations: Insects and spiders have evolved a stunning variety of adaptations that enable them to thrive in their respective environments. Insects exhibit diverse wing shapes, mouthparts, and camouflage strategies that facilitate survival and reproduction. Similarly, spiders have evolved various types of silk, venomous fangs, and sensory structures that aid in hunting, defense, and navigation.

Ecological Niches: From pollinating plants to controlling pest populations, insects play critical roles in ecosystems. Bees, for instance, are essential pollinators for flowering plants, while ants are efficient scavengers that contribute to nutrient recycling. Spiders, on the other hand, help control insect populations, preventing outbreaks that could disrupt ecosystem balance.

Unearthing Biodiversity: Scientists and entomologists continue to make astounding discoveries about new insect and spider species. Exploring remote rainforests, investigating the depths of caves, and even studying the microhabitats of urban environments reveal previously unknown species that enrich our understanding of Earth's biodiversity.

Conservation Concerns: Despite their essential contributions to ecosystems, insects and spiders face challenges such as habitat loss, climate change, and pollution. Conservation efforts are crucial to safeguard their populations and the services they provide to both natural and human-made environments.

Cultural Significance: Insects and spiders have captured human imagination for centuries, inspiring art, mythology, and cultural symbolism. They have been revered as symbols of transformation, perseverance, and even spiritual significance in various cultures around the world.

A Journey Through Diversity: As we embark on a journey through the world of insects and spiders, we will explore the vast array of species, behaviors, and ecological interactions that make up this intricate tapestry of life. From the microscopic world of ants to the impressive silk-spinning abilities of orb-weaving spiders, our exploration will uncover the beauty and complexity of these creatures that share our planet.

Behavioral adaptations and ecological roles

Behavioral Adaptations and Ecological Roles of Insects and Spiders

The behavioral adaptations of insects and spiders are nothing short of remarkable, enabling them to thrive in diverse ecological niches and play crucial roles in ecosystems worldwide. From intricate mating rituals to cooperative behaviors, these adaptations are essential for their survival and their contributions to the balance of the natural world.

Behavioral Adaptations:

1. **Camouflage and Mimicry:** Many insects and spiders have evolved the ability to blend into their surroundings through coloration, shape, and behavior. Camouflage allows them to evade predators or ambush prey, while mimicry involves imitating other organisms or objects for protection.

2. **Social Behavior:** Some insects, like ants, bees, and termites, exhibit complex social structures. They live in colonies with specialized roles such as workers, soldiers, and reproductive individuals. Cooperation within these colonies ensures the survival and success of the group.

3. **Communication:** Insects and spiders communicate using a variety of cues, including visual, auditory, and chemical signals. This communication helps them find mates, establish territories, and warn others of danger.

4. **Parental Care:** Some insects and spiders provide care for their offspring. For example, female spiders may

guard their egg sacs, and certain beetle species engage in parental care by protecting and providing food for their developing larvae.

5. **Predator-Prey Interactions:** Insects and spiders have evolved diverse hunting and defense strategies. Predatory insects like mantises and dragonflies use stealth or speed to catch prey, while defensive behaviors such as playing dead or releasing noxious chemicals deter predators.

Ecological Roles:

1. **Pollination:** Insects, particularly bees and butterflies, play a crucial role in pollinating flowering plants. This process is essential for plant reproduction and the production of fruits and seeds, which many other animals depend on for food.

2. **Decomposition:** Insects like beetles and flies are essential decomposers, breaking down organic matter and recycling nutrients back into the ecosystem. Without them, dead organisms and waste would accumulate, disrupting nutrient cycles.

3. **Pest Control:** Predatory insects, spiders, and insectivorous birds help control populations of pest species. This natural pest control reduces the need for chemical pesticides and helps maintain ecosystem balance.

4. **Food Source:** Insects and spiders are a crucial food source for numerous animals, including birds, reptiles, amphibians, and mammals. They serve as a link in the food chain, supporting higher trophic levels.

5. **Nutrient Cycling:** Insects that feed on plants, such as caterpillars and grasshoppers, help regulate plant growth and maintain the balance of plant communities. They prevent overgrowth and contribute to nutrient cycling.

6. **Ecosystem Engineers:** Some insects, like ants, modify their environment by creating nests, tunnels, and mounds. These modifications influence soil structure and nutrient distribution, impacting ecosystem dynamics.

A Delicate Balance: The behavioral adaptations of insects and spiders enable them to fill specific ecological roles within their habitats. Their interactions with plants, other animals, and the environment contribute to the intricate web of life. Understanding these roles is vital for conservation efforts, as disruptions to insect and spider populations can have cascading effects on entire ecosystems.

Impact on ecosystems and human society

Impact of Insects and Spiders on Ecosystems and Human Society

Insects and spiders, with their diverse behavioral adaptations and ecological roles, have profound impacts on both ecosystems and human society. These small creatures play essential roles in maintaining ecosystem health, supporting agriculture, and contributing to scientific research. However, their presence can also lead to challenges, such as disease transmission and crop damage.

Ecosystem Impact:

1. **Pollination and Biodiversity:** Insects, especially bees and butterflies, are vital pollinators of flowering plants. They facilitate the reproduction of many plant species, which in turn supports biodiversity by providing habitat and food for other organisms.
2. **Decomposition and Nutrient Cycling:** Insects and spiders contribute to nutrient cycling by breaking down organic matter and returning essential nutrients to the soil. This process enhances soil fertility and supports plant growth.
3. **Food Web Dynamics:** Insects and spiders form the base of many food webs, providing nutrition to a wide range of predators. Their abundance or scarcity can influence the population dynamics of higher trophic levels, including birds, reptiles, and mammals.
4. **Ecosystem Engineers:** Insects like ants and termites modify their environment by building nests and

tunnels. These structures create microhabitats and influence soil composition, benefiting the overall ecosystem.

Agricultural and Economic Impact:

1. **Crop Pollination:** Insects play a crucial role in pollinating crops that contribute significantly to human nutrition, including fruits, vegetables, and nuts. Pollination by bees alone is estimated to enhance global crop value by billions of dollars annually.

2. **Pest Control:** Predatory insects and spiders help control pest populations in agriculture. This natural pest control reduces the need for chemical pesticides, promoting more sustainable farming practices.

3. **Silk Production:** Certain insects, like silkworms, produce materials of economic value. Silk, produced by silkworm larvae, has been used for centuries to create fabrics and textiles.

4. **Honey Production:** Bees produce honey, a nutritious and sweet substance that has both culinary and medicinal uses. Honey production supports local economies and livelihoods.

Challenges and Risks:

1. **Disease Vectors:** Some insects, such as mosquitoes, can transmit diseases to humans and animals. Malaria, Zika virus, and dengue fever are examples of diseases spread by mosquitoes.

2. **Crop Damage:** While insects play a positive role in agriculture, certain species can also damage crops by feeding on plants or transmitting plant diseases. This can lead to economic losses for farmers.

3. **Invasive Species:** Invasive insects, when introduced to new areas, can disrupt ecosystems by outcompeting native species, damaging crops, and impacting

wildlife.

4. **Allergies:** Some people are allergic to insect stings or bites, which can lead to severe reactions or health issues.

Scientific and Ecological Research:

1. **Bioindicators:** Changes in insect and spider populations can indicate shifts in ecosystem health. Monitoring these populations can provide valuable insights into environmental changes.
2. **Behavioral Studies:** Insects and spiders offer valuable opportunities for studying behavior, communication, and social structures. These studies contribute to our understanding of animal behavior and cognition.

In conclusion, the impact of insects and spiders on ecosystems and human society is multifaceted. Their roles in pollination, decomposition, and nutrient cycling are essential for maintaining ecosystem balance and supporting agricultural production. However, challenges such as disease transmission and crop damage remind us of the delicate balance between the benefits and risks associated with these creatures. As we strive to conserve biodiversity and address global challenges, understanding the intricate roles of insects and spiders remains a critical endeavor.

Mammalia: Mammals

Diversity and Significance of Mammals

Mammals, a class of vertebrate animals, exhibit a remarkable diversity of forms, behaviors, and ecological roles. They are characterized by features such as mammary glands, hair or fur, and the ability to regulate their body temperature. Mammals play vital roles in ecosystems, have unique physiological adaptations, and have developed complex behaviors and social structures.

Mammal Diversity:

1. **Classification:** Mammals are classified into various orders, including primates, rodents, carnivores, cetaceans, and more. This classification is based on anatomical, physiological, and genetic characteristics.
2. **Terrestrial and Aquatic:** Mammals inhabit a wide range of environments, from terrestrial ecosystems like forests and grasslands to aquatic habitats such as oceans, rivers, and lakes.

Ecological Roles:

1. **Predators and Prey:** Mammals occupy different trophic levels in food chains and food webs. Some are apex predators that regulate prey populations, while others serve as prey for larger predators.
2. **Herbivores and Plant Dispersers:** Many mammals are herbivores that graze on plants, shaping plant communities and contributing to seed dispersal as they move between feeding areas.

3. **Pollinators:** Bats and some small mammals play a role in pollination, aiding in the reproduction of flowering plants and ensuring ecosystem biodiversity.

Physiological Adaptations:

1. **Thermoregulation:** Mammals have a high metabolic rate and can regulate their body temperature through mechanisms like sweating, panting, and insulation provided by fur or fat.
2. **Mammary Glands:** Female mammals possess mammary glands that produce milk, allowing them to nourish their young.

Behavior and Social Structures:

1. **Communication:** Mammals communicate using various vocalizations, body language, and chemical signals. These signals are vital for social interactions, mating, and defense.
2. **Parental Care:** Many mammals provide extensive parental care to their offspring, ensuring their survival through feeding, protection, and teaching essential skills.
3. **Social Groups:** Mammals exhibit a range of social structures, from solitary individuals to complex social groups like prides, packs, and troops. These structures facilitate cooperation, protection, and resource sharing.

Human Interaction:

1. **Domestication:** Humans have domesticated several mammal species for various purposes, including transportation, labor, companionship, and food production.
2. **Conservation:** Mammals face threats such as habitat loss, climate change, and poaching. Conservation

efforts aim to protect endangered species and their habitats.

Iconic Mammals:

1. **Primates:** Primates, including humans, are known for their advanced cognitive abilities, tool use, and complex social behaviors.
2. **Cetaceans:** Dolphins and whales are cetaceans, known for their intelligence and sophisticated communication skills.
3. **Carnivores:** Lions, tigers, wolves, and other carnivores are apex predators that play essential roles in maintaining ecosystem balance.
4. **Rodents:** Rodents like rats, mice, and squirrels are highly adaptable and inhabit various environments worldwide.

Future Challenges:

1. **Biodiversity Loss:** As habitats continue to be threatened by human activities, many mammal species are at risk of extinction. Conservation efforts are crucial to preserving biodiversity.
2. **Climate Change:** Mammals, particularly those with specific habitat requirements, may be vulnerable to the effects of climate change, such as altered temperature patterns and shifts in food availability.

In conclusion, mammals are a diverse and essential group of animals with significant ecological, physiological, and behavioral roles. From apex predators to herbivores and pollinators, they shape ecosystems and contribute to the functioning of the natural world. Understanding and conserving mammal species are critical for maintaining biodiversity, ecological balance, and the intricate web of life on Earth.

Diverse characteristics of mammals

Mammals exhibit a wide range of characteristics that set them apart from other animal groups. These characteristics contribute to their remarkable diversity and adaptability to various environments. Here are some diverse characteristics of mammals:

1. **Hair or Fur:** Mammals possess hair or fur on their bodies, which serves multiple functions, including insulation, camouflage, and sensory perception.
2. **Mammary Glands:** All female mammals have mammary glands that produce milk to nourish their young. This unique feature supports the care and development of offspring.
3. **Endothermy:** Mammals are endothermic, meaning they can regulate their body temperature internally. This ability allows them to thrive in diverse habitats, including cold and hot environments.
4. **Four-Chambered Hearts:** Mammals have four-chambered hearts, which efficiently pump oxygenated and deoxygenated blood, ensuring effective oxygen delivery to body tissues.
5. **Diverse Dentition:** Mammals possess a variety of teeth adapted to their diets. Different types of teeth, such as incisors, canines, premolars, and molars, enable them to consume a wide range of foods.
6. **Highly Developed Brains:** Mammals have well-developed brains relative to their body size. This complexity is associated with advanced cognitive abilities, problem-solving, and social behaviors.

7. **Internal Fertilization:** Most mammals reproduce through internal fertilization, where the male's sperm fertilizes the female's eggs inside her body.

8. **Live Birth:** While some mammals lay eggs (monotremes and marsupials), most give birth to live young. The young are born at various stages of development, ranging from relatively undeveloped to fully formed.

9. **Complex Behavior:** Mammals display a wide range of behaviors, from intricate social interactions to complex feeding strategies and communication methods.

10. **Variety of Locomotion:** Mammals exhibit diverse forms of locomotion, including walking, running, climbing, swimming, and flying (bats).

11. **Diverse Diets:** Mammals consume a variety of diets, including herbivores (plant-eaters), carnivores (meat-eaters), omnivores (both plant and animal eaters), and insectivores (insect eaters).

12. **Specialized Appendages:** Mammals have evolved specialized adaptations, such as hooves, claws, wings, and prehensile tails, to suit their lifestyles and ecological niches.

13. **Echolocation:** Some mammals, such as bats and cetaceans (whales and dolphins), use echolocation to navigate and locate prey in their environments.

14. **Various Reproductive Strategies:** Mammals exhibit diverse reproductive strategies, including monogamy, polygamy, and various mating rituals.

15. **Social Structures:** Mammals live in a wide range of social structures, including solitary, pair-bonded, family groups, and complex societies with hierarchies.

16. **Sensory Perception:** Mammals have well-developed sensory organs, including keen senses of sight, hearing, and smell, which contribute to their ability to detect and respond to their surroundings.

The diversity of these characteristics showcases the adaptability of mammals to various ecological niches and their complex interactions with other organisms and the environment.

Adaptations for various habitats

Mammals have evolved a wide range of adaptations that allow them to thrive in diverse habitats around the world. These adaptations help them meet the specific challenges and demands of their environments. Here are some examples of adaptations for various habitats:

1. **Terrestrial Habitats:**
   - **Deserts:** Desert-dwelling mammals, such as camels and kangaroo rats, have evolved specialized kidneys and adaptations to minimize water loss.
   - **Forests:** Arboreal mammals like squirrels and primates have prehensile tails and strong limb adaptations for climbing and maneuvering in trees.
   - **Grasslands:** Herbivorous mammals like zebras and bison have evolved large, flat teeth for efficient grinding of grasses.
2. **Aquatic Habitats:**
   - **Marine Mammals:** Whales, dolphins, and seals have streamlined bodies, flippers, and blubber for efficient swimming and insulation in cold water.
   - **Semi-Aquatic Mammals:** Animals like otters and beavers have webbed feet and dense fur to help them swim and regulate body temperature.
3. **Underground Habitats:**
   - **Burrowing Mammals:** Animals like moles

and gophers have strong forelimbs and adapted claws for digging burrows and tunnels.

4. **Nocturnal Habitats:**

   - **Nocturnal Adaptations:** Animals like owls and bats have specialized senses, such as acute hearing and echolocation, to navigate and hunt in the dark.

5. **Arctic and Antarctic Habitats:**

   - **Insulation:** Arctic mammals like polar bears have thick layers of blubber and fur to insulate against the cold.
   - **Counter-Current Heat Exchange:** Some marine mammals have counter-current heat exchange systems that prevent heat loss in extremities while swimming in cold water.

6. **High Altitude Habitats:**

   - **High Altitude Adaptations:** Animals like the Himalayan tahr have adapted to low oxygen levels by developing efficient respiratory and circulatory systems.

7. **Caves:**

   - **Nocturnal and Blind Adaptations:** Many cave-dwelling mammals are nocturnal and may have reduced or absent eyes due to the lack of light.

8. **Camouflage and Mimicry:**

   - **Camouflage:** Some mammals have evolved fur patterns that help them blend into their environments, making them less visible to predators or prey.
   - **Mimicry:** Certain mammals use mimicry to resemble other animals, helping them avoid predators or gain access to resources.

9. **Migratory Habits:**

   - **Migration:** Many mammals, such as caribou

and wildebeest, undertake long-distance migrations to access food, avoid harsh weather, or give birth in safer areas.

10. **Social Structures:**
   - **Group Living:** Some mammals, like meerkats and African elephants, form social groups for protection, resource sharing, and cooperative care of young.

These adaptations demonstrate the incredible diversity of mammalian species and their ability to adapt to a wide range of habitats. Each adaptation is a result of evolutionary processes that have allowed mammals to survive and thrive in their respective environments.

Conservation challenges and success stories

Conservation efforts for mammals face numerous challenges due to factors such as habitat loss, pollution, climate change, poaching, and human-wildlife conflicts. Despite these challenges, there have been several success stories that highlight the positive impact of conservation initiatives. Here are some conservation challenges and success stories related to mammal species:

Challenges:

1. **Habitat Loss:** Many mammal species are threatened by the destruction and fragmentation of their habitats due to urbanization, deforestation, and agricultural expansion.
2. **Poaching:** Illegal hunting for fur, body parts, and the exotic pet trade poses a significant threat to various mammal species, especially those with high commercial value.
3. **Climate Change:** Changing climatic conditions can affect mammal habitats, food availability, and migration patterns, leading to shifts in distribution and behavior.
4. **Human-Wildlife Conflict:** Conflicts between humans and mammals, such as predators preying on livestock, can lead to retaliatory killings and endanger the survival of certain species.
5. **Invasive Species:** Invasive species can outcompete native mammals for resources and introduce new diseases, leading to declines in native populations.

Success Stories:

1. **Giant Panda Conservation:** Conservation efforts for giant pandas in China have led to increased protection of their bamboo forest habitats, captive breeding programs, and successful reintroduction into the wild.
2. **Black Rhino Recovery:** The conservation of black rhinos has shown progress through anti-poaching efforts, habitat restoration, and translocation programs, leading to a gradual increase in their numbers.
3. **Gray Wolf Recovery:** Conservation efforts have led to the recovery of gray wolf populations in parts of North America and Europe, thanks to legal protection, reintroduction programs, and public support.
4. **Mountain Gorilla Conservation:** Collaborative conservation efforts have helped stabilize and increase mountain gorilla populations through protected areas, anti-poaching patrols, and ecotourism.
5. **Cheetah Conservation:** Conservation programs for cheetahs involve research, education, and efforts to mitigate human-wildlife conflicts, which have contributed to the protection of these vulnerable big cats.
6. **Snow Leopard Conservation:** Conservation initiatives are focused on protecting snow leopard habitats, reducing poaching, and promoting community-based conservation in their range countries.

These examples showcase the potential for successful conservation when governments, organizations, communities, and individuals work together to address challenges and protect mammal species. While there is still much work to be done, these success stories inspire hope for the future of mammal conservation.

Reptilia & Amphibia: Reptiles & Amphibians

Reptiles and amphibians are diverse groups of cold-blooded vertebrates that inhabit a wide range of terrestrial, aquatic, and semi-aquatic environments. They play important roles in ecosystems as predators, prey, and indicators of environmental health. Here is an overview of the characteristics, diversity, adaptations, and conservation considerations for reptiles and amphibians:

Characteristics of Reptiles:

- Reptiles include snakes, lizards, turtles, crocodiles, and tuataras.
- They have dry, scaly skin that helps prevent water loss.
- Reptiles lay eggs with leathery or hard shells, and most undergo internal fertilization.
- They are ectothermic, meaning their body temperature is regulated by the environment.
- Many reptiles have specialized adaptations, such as venomous glands in snakes and protective shells in turtles.

Characteristics of Amphibians:

- Amphibians include frogs, toads, salamanders, and newts.
- They have moist, permeable skin that allows for respiration through the skin.
- Amphibians usually lay eggs in water, and most have a

larval aquatic stage (tadpoles).
- They are ectothermic, but their reliance on external water sources makes them sensitive to environmental changes.

Adaptations:

- Reptiles have evolved various adaptations to thrive in different environments. For example, chameleons have specialized tongues for catching insects, and crocodiles have powerful jaws for hunting.
- Amphibians have unique reproductive strategies, such as external fertilization and metamorphosis from aquatic larvae to terrestrial adults.
- Both groups have developed camouflage, warning coloration, and other defensive mechanisms to avoid predators.

Conservation Concerns:

- Reptiles and amphibians are vulnerable to habitat loss, pollution, climate change, and disease.
- Chytrid fungus has decimated amphibian populations globally.
- Many reptiles are harvested for their skins, meat, and body parts, contributing to population declines.
- Invasive species, habitat destruction, and pollution threaten their survival.

Conservation Efforts:

- Protected areas, habitat restoration, and anti-poaching efforts are crucial for conserving reptiles and amphibians.
- Captive breeding and reintroduction programs help boost populations of endangered species.
- Public education and awareness campaigns promote conservation and reduce demand for wildlife

products.

- International agreements and laws, such as the Convention on International Trade in Endangered Species of Wild Fauna and Flora (CITES), regulate trade in reptiles and amphibians.

Reptiles and amphibians are integral components of ecosystems, playing roles in nutrient cycling, pest control, and biodiversity. Conservation efforts are essential to ensure the survival of these fascinating and diverse creatures for future generations.

Distinctive features of reptiles and amphibians

Reptiles and amphibians are two distinct groups of cold-blooded vertebrates with unique features that differentiate them from each other and from other animal groups. Here are some of the distinctive features of reptiles and amphibians:

Reptiles:

1. **Scaly Skin:** Reptiles are known for their dry, scaly skin that helps prevent water loss. The scales are made of keratin, the same material found in human hair and nails.
2. **Lungs:** Reptiles have well-developed lungs that allow them to breathe air. They have a more efficient respiratory system compared to amphibians.
3. **Ectothermy:** Reptiles are ectothermic, meaning their body temperature is regulated by external environmental conditions. They rely on external sources of heat, such as the sun, to maintain their body temperature.
4. **Shelled Eggs:** Reptiles lay eggs with tough, leathery, or calcified shells that protect the developing embryos from desiccation and predation.
5. **Internal Fertilization:** Most reptiles practice internal fertilization, where males deposit sperm directly into the female's reproductive tract.
6. **Three-Chambered Heart:** Reptiles typically have a three-chambered heart with two atria and one ventricle, which helps to partially separate oxygenated and deoxygenated blood.
7. **Oviparous:** Most reptiles are oviparous, meaning

they lay eggs that hatch outside the mother's body. However, some reptiles, like some species of snakes and lizards, give birth to live young.

Amphibians:

1. **Moist Skin:** Amphibians have thin, moist, permeable skin that allows them to exchange gases and absorb moisture directly from their environment. Their skin is highly sensitive to environmental changes.
2. **Bimodal Respiration:** Amphibians can respire through their skin, in addition to using lungs or gills, depending on their life stage and habitat.
3. **Metamorphosis:** Many amphibians undergo metamorphosis, a dramatic transformation from aquatic larvae to terrestrial adults. This process often involves changes in body structure, behavior, and habitat.
4. **Aquatic Larvae:** Most amphibians lay eggs in water, and their eggs hatch into aquatic larvae, such as tadpoles. These larvae eventually undergo metamorphosis to become adults adapted to terrestrial life.
5. **Dual Life Habitats:** Amphibians often have dual life stages, spending part of their lives in water as larvae and part on land as adults. This dual life strategy connects aquatic and terrestrial ecosystems.
6. **Sensitive Indicator Species:** Amphibians are sensitive to environmental changes, making them important indicator species. Declines in amphibian populations can signal changes in ecosystem health.
7. **External Fertilization:** Many amphibians practice external fertilization, where males release sperm onto the eggs after they are laid by the female.

These distinctive features reflect the adaptations that reptiles and amphibians have developed to thrive in various environments. While both groups share the common ancestry of vertebrates, they have evolved unique traits that have allowed them to occupy diverse ecological niches and contribute to the biodiversity of our planet.

Reproduction strategies and habitats

Reproduction Strategies:

Reptiles: Reptiles exhibit a variety of reproductive strategies depending on the species. Some common reproduction strategies among reptiles include:

1. **Oviparous:** Many reptiles are oviparous, meaning they lay eggs. The eggs are usually laid in a safe location, where they are protected from predators and environmental conditions. The embryo develops inside the egg, and the young hatch from the eggs when they are fully developed.
2. **Viviparous:** Some reptile species are viviparous, meaning they give birth to live young. In viviparous species, the embryos develop within the mother's body, and the young are born fully formed.
3. **Ovoviviparous:** This strategy combines aspects of both oviparous and viviparous reproduction. In ovoviviparous species, the embryos develop within eggs that remain inside the mother's body until they are ready to hatch. The young are then born as live offspring.

Amphibians: Amphibians also exhibit diverse reproduction strategies based on their life stages and habitats:

1. **External Fertilization:** Many amphibians practice external fertilization, where males release sperm onto the eggs after they are laid by the female. This typically occurs in aquatic environments, as the eggs and sperm

need to meet in water for fertilization.

2. **Aquatic Eggs:** Most amphibians lay eggs in water, where the eggs develop into aquatic larvae, such as tadpoles. These larvae go through metamorphosis and transition to a terrestrial adult form.

3. **Parental Care:** Some amphibian species exhibit parental care, where adults guard and protect the eggs or young. For example, male frogs may guard the eggs laid by females to prevent predation.

Habitats:

Reptiles: Reptiles inhabit a wide range of habitats, including deserts, forests, grasslands, wetlands, and aquatic environments. Their adaptations to specific habitats can vary widely. For example, desert-dwelling reptiles often have adaptations to conserve water, while aquatic reptiles have adaptations for swimming and catching prey in water.

Amphibians: Amphibians are closely tied to aquatic environments, especially during their larval stages. Many amphibians, such as frogs and salamanders, lay their eggs in water bodies like ponds, lakes, and streams. The larvae develop in water and go through metamorphosis to become terrestrial adults. However, some amphibians, like certain salamanders, remain aquatic throughout their lives.

It's important to note that both reptiles and amphibians are highly diverse groups with species adapted to a wide range of habitats and reproductive strategies. Their reproductive and habitat preferences are influenced by factors such as climate, food availability, predation pressures, and evolutionary history.

Conservation efforts and habitat protection

Conservation Efforts and Habitat Protection for Reptiles and Amphibians:

Conserving reptiles and amphibians is crucial for maintaining biodiversity and the health of ecosystems. These animals play important roles in their habitats as both predators and prey, and they contribute to various ecological processes. However, many reptile and amphibian species are facing population declines and are listed as threatened or endangered. Conservation efforts and habitat protection are essential to ensure their survival. Here are some key conservation strategies:

1. **Habitat Protection:** Protecting natural habitats is a primary focus of conservation efforts. Designating and managing protected areas, such as national parks and wildlife reserves, helps preserve essential habitats for reptiles and amphibians. Conserving wetlands, forests, grasslands, and aquatic environments is crucial for these animals.

2. **Restoration:** Restoration projects aim to restore degraded habitats to their natural conditions. This may involve removing invasive species, restoring waterways, and replanting native vegetation. By restoring habitats, conservationists provide suitable homes for reptiles and amphibians to thrive.

3. **Anti-Poaching Measures:** Illegal collection and trade of reptiles and amphibians for the pet trade can threaten their populations. Enforcing anti-poaching measures and regulations on the trade of these animals can help curb illegal activities that contribute

to their decline.

4. **Public Awareness and Education:** Raising awareness among local communities and the general public about the importance of reptiles and amphibians is crucial. Educating people about the role these animals play in ecosystems and the consequences of their decline can garner support for conservation efforts.

5. **Breeding Programs:** Captive breeding programs are established to breed and raise reptiles and amphibians in controlled environments. These programs can help supplement wild populations and provide individuals for reintroduction into the wild.

6. **Research and Monitoring:** Conducting scientific research on reptile and amphibian populations helps monitor their health and population trends. Understanding their habitats, behaviors, and threats is essential for effective conservation planning.

7. **Reintroduction:** Reintroducing captive-bred individuals into their natural habitats can help boost populations that have declined. However, successful reintroduction requires careful planning and consideration of factors such as habitat quality and disease risk.

8. **Collaboration:** Collaboration among governments, non-governmental organizations (NGOs), scientists, local communities, and other stakeholders is crucial for effective conservation efforts. Working together can lead to more comprehensive and impactful initiatives.

9. **Climate Change Mitigation:** Addressing climate change is vital for the long-term survival of reptiles and amphibians. As temperature and precipitation patterns shift, habitats may become less suitable for these animals. Efforts to reduce greenhouse gas emissions and adapt to changing conditions can benefit their conservation.

Conserving reptiles and amphibians requires a multifaceted approach that considers their specific ecological needs, threats, and the unique challenges they face. By implementing effective conservation strategies, we can contribute to the preservation of these valuable and ecologically important creatures.

Wildlife and Conservation

Wildlife and Conservation:

Wildlife conservation is a critical endeavor aimed at protecting and preserving the Earth's diverse range of animal species and their habitats. Wildlife plays a crucial role in maintaining ecological balance and contributes to the overall health and functioning of ecosystems. However, human activities, habitat loss, pollution, climate change, and poaching have led to the decline of many wildlife populations. Conservation efforts are essential to prevent further species loss and to ensure the continued health of the planet's biodiversity.

Importance of Wildlife Conservation:

1. **Biodiversity:** Wildlife represents a vast diversity of species, each with unique characteristics and roles in ecosystems. Biodiversity contributes to ecosystem stability, resilience, and productivity.
2. **Ecological Balance:** Predators help control prey populations, herbivores shape plant communities, and scavengers clean up organic matter. Maintaining these interactions is crucial for ecosystem health.
3. **Ecosystem Services:** Wildlife provides valuable ecosystem services such as pollination, seed dispersal, and nutrient cycling that benefit both natural habitats and human activities like agriculture.
4. **Scientific Research:** Studying wildlife helps us understand the complexities of ecosystems, genetics, behavior, and evolution. This knowledge informs various fields, including medicine and conservation

biology.

5. **Cultural and Aesthetic Value:** Wildlife has cultural significance and contributes to the aesthetic enjoyment of nature. Many people find solace, inspiration, and recreational opportunities in observing and interacting with wildlife.

Wildlife Conservation Strategies:

1. **Habitat Protection:** Preserving natural habitats is the foundation of wildlife conservation. Protected areas, national parks, and wildlife reserves provide safe havens for a wide range of species.
2. **Habitat Restoration:** Restoring degraded habitats through reforestation, wetland rehabilitation, and invasive species removal helps improve conditions for wildlife.
3. **Anti-Poaching Efforts:** Poaching for illegal wildlife trade threatens many species. Enforcing anti-poaching laws and increasing penalties for illegal activities are crucial to combat this threat.
4. **Community Involvement:** Engaging local communities in conservation efforts fosters a sense of ownership and responsibility. Sustainable resource management and ecotourism can provide economic incentives for conservation.
5. **Education and Awareness:** Educating the public about the importance of wildlife conservation and the impact of human activities is essential for garnering support for conservation initiatives.
6. **Research and Monitoring:** Scientific research helps us understand species' behavior, ecology, and population trends. Monitoring programs provide data to guide conservation decisions.
7. **Reintroduction and Translocation:** Reintroducing or translocating species to their historical ranges can

help restore populations that have declined.

8. **Global Cooperation:** Many species migrate across borders. International collaboration is crucial for protecting migratory species and addressing global conservation challenges.

9. **Climate Change Mitigation:** Addressing climate change is essential for wildlife conservation. Protecting habitats, reducing emissions, and promoting adaptation strategies can help safeguard species.

Wildlife conservation is a shared responsibility that requires cooperation among governments, organizations, communities, and individuals. By working together to protect and conserve wildlife, we can ensure a sustainable and vibrant planet for current and future generations.

Biodiversity hotspots and endangered species

Biodiversity Hotspots and Endangered Species:

Biodiversity hotspots are regions of the world that contain exceptionally high levels of species diversity and are under significant threat due to habitat loss and degradation. These areas are crucial for conserving biodiversity as they harbor a large number of unique and endemic species that are found nowhere else on Earth. Biodiversity hotspots are a priority for conservation efforts because their protection can have a disproportionately positive impact on global biodiversity conservation.

Characteristics of Biodiversity Hotspots:

1. **High Species Diversity:** Biodiversity hotspots are characterized by a high number of species, including plants, animals, and microorganisms. These species have evolved in these areas over millions of years, resulting in unique adaptations and ecological interactions.

2. **Endemic Species:** Many species found in biodiversity hotspots are endemic, meaning they are not found anywhere else in the world. This makes these regions especially important for preserving evolutionary history.

3. **Threats to Habitats:** Biodiversity hotspots often face threats such as deforestation, habitat fragmentation, pollution, climate change, and invasive species. These threats can lead to the loss of species and ecological disruption.

Endangered Species in Biodiversity Hotspots:

1. **Endangered and Critically Endangered Species:** Biodiversity hotspots are home to many species that are classified as endangered or critically endangered by the International Union for Conservation of Nature (IUCN). These species face a high risk of extinction due to the loss of their habitats.

2. **Amphibians:** Biodiversity hotspots, particularly tropical rainforests, are home to a significant number of amphibian species. Many amphibians are facing population declines due to habitat destruction and the spread of a fungal disease called chytridiomycosis.

3. **Plants:** Biodiversity hotspots often have rich plant diversity, with many unique plant species. Habitat destruction and illegal trade in plants can threaten these species.

4. **Mammals and Birds:** Endemic mammals and birds in hotspots can be vulnerable to habitat loss and hunting.

Conservation Efforts in Biodiversity Hotspots:

1. **Protected Areas:** Establishing and maintaining protected areas, such as national parks and reserves, is crucial for preserving the unique biodiversity of hotspots.

2. **Habitat Restoration:** Efforts to restore degraded habitats within hotspots can help provide suitable conditions for endangered species.

3. **Community Involvement:** Engaging local communities in conservation efforts ensures that their needs are met while conserving biodiversity. Sustainable livelihoods and ecotourism can provide economic incentives.

4. **Scientific Research:** Research on endemic and threatened species within hotspots can inform

conservation strategies and management plans.

5. **International Collaboration:** Many hotspots span multiple countries, requiring international cooperation to address conservation challenges.
6. **Education and Advocacy:** Raising awareness about the importance of biodiversity hotspots and the species they contain can lead to increased public support for conservation efforts.
7. **Funding and Resources:** Providing financial resources and support to conservation organizations working in hotspots is essential for implementing effective conservation measures.

Biodiversity hotspots are critical areas for both preserving Earth's natural heritage and supporting the ecological health of the planet. By focusing conservation efforts on these regions, we can work to prevent the loss of unique species and maintain the delicate balance of ecosystems.

Role of protected areas and conservation organizations

Role of Protected Areas and Conservation Organizations:

Protected areas and conservation organizations play a crucial role in safeguarding the world's biodiversity and natural ecosystems. They are essential components of global efforts to address habitat loss, species extinction, and environmental degradation. These entities work together to create a network of conservation strategies that aim to protect and sustainably manage the Earth's natural resources for current and future generations.

Protected Areas:

1. **Habitat Preservation:** Protected areas, such as national parks, wildlife sanctuaries, and marine reserves, serve as safe havens for biodiversity by preserving natural habitats and ecosystems. They provide critical spaces where native plants and animals can thrive without the pressures of human development.

2. **Biodiversity Conservation:** These areas are designed to conserve a wide range of species, including endangered, endemic, and keystone species. By protecting these species, protected areas contribute to overall ecosystem health and resilience.

3. **Scientific Research:** Protected areas provide opportunities for scientific research and monitoring of ecosystems, species behavior, and environmental

changes. Research conducted in these areas contributes to our understanding of biodiversity, ecology, and natural processes.

4. **Education and Recreation:** Protected areas offer opportunities for environmental education, nature-based tourism, and recreational activities. These activities promote awareness of the value of biodiversity and foster a connection between people and nature.

5. **Climate Change Mitigation:** Many protected areas, especially forests and wetlands, play a vital role in carbon sequestration and climate regulation. These areas can help mitigate the impacts of climate change by absorbing carbon dioxide and providing other ecosystem services.

Conservation Organizations:

1. **Research and Advocacy:** Conservation organizations conduct scientific research to understand the threats to biodiversity and develop effective conservation strategies. They advocate for policies and laws that protect natural resources and habitats.

2. **Habitat Restoration:** Conservation organizations work on restoring degraded habitats through initiatives such as reforestation, wetland restoration, and invasive species removal. Restoration efforts enhance habitat quality and support the return of native species.

3. **Species Protection:** These organizations focus on protecting endangered species by implementing breeding programs, monitoring populations, and mitigating threats such as poaching and habitat loss.

4. **Community Engagement:** Many conservation organizations engage with local communities to ensure that conservation efforts are aligned with

community needs and provide sustainable livelihoods. This approach fosters support and stewardship from local populations.

5. **Capacity Building:** Conservation organizations build local and global capacity through training programs, workshops, and collaborations with governments, communities, and other stakeholders.

6. **Funding and Fundraising:** Conservation organizations raise funds from various sources, including donations, grants, and partnerships, to support their conservation projects and initiatives.

7. **Public Awareness:** These organizations raise public awareness about the importance of biodiversity, environmental conservation, and sustainable living. They educate people about the impacts of their actions on nature and promote behavior changes that support conservation.

Collaboration Between Protected Areas and Conservation Organizations:

Protected areas often collaborate with conservation organizations to implement effective management plans, research initiatives, and community engagement activities. Conservation organizations provide resources, expertise, and technical support to enhance the conservation efforts of protected areas. This collaboration results in a synergistic approach that addresses conservation challenges comprehensively.

Overall, the combined efforts of protected areas and conservation organizations are essential for maintaining the planet's ecological balance, preserving biodiversity, and ensuring the well-being of both natural ecosystems and human societies.

Human impact on wildlife and ethical considerations

Human Impact on Wildlife and Ethical Considerations:

Human activities have a significant impact on wildlife and their habitats, often leading to habitat destruction, species extinction, and ecological imbalances. Ethical considerations come into play when assessing the moral responsibilities humans have towards the natural world and its inhabitants. Understanding these impacts and considering ethical principles is crucial for promoting conservation, sustainability, and coexistence with wildlife.

Human Impact on Wildlife:

1. **Habitat Loss and Fragmentation:** Urbanization, deforestation, agriculture, and infrastructure development lead to the destruction and fragmentation of habitats. This disrupts ecosystems, displaces species, and reduces biodiversity.
2. **Pollution:** Pollution from industrial, agricultural, and urban sources contaminates water bodies, air, and soil, posing serious threats to wildlife health and survival. Chemical pollutants can accumulate in the food chain, causing long-term harm.
3. **Climate Change:** Human-induced climate change alters habitats, disrupts migration patterns, and affects the availability of food and resources. Rising temperatures and extreme weather events directly impact species' survival and reproduction.

4. **Overexploitation:** Overhunting, overfishing, and illegal wildlife trade threaten species with extinction. Unsustainable exploitation disrupts ecosystems and disrupts the balance of predator-prey relationships.
5. **Invasive Species:** Human introduction of non-native species can outcompete native species, disrupt ecosystems, and lead to declines in local biodiversity.
6. **Habitat Degradation:** Activities like mining, logging, and agriculture degrade habitats and reduce the quality of ecosystems, affecting species' ability to thrive.

Ethical Considerations:

1. **Intrinsic Value of Wildlife:** Ethical arguments recognize that wildlife has inherent value and a right to exist regardless of their utility to humans. This perspective emphasizes the intrinsic worth of all living beings.
2. **Stewardship:** Humans are stewards of the Earth and have a responsibility to care for and protect all species and ecosystems. This stewardship approach emphasizes our moral duty to prevent harm to wildlife.
3. **Biodiversity Conservation:** Recognizing the importance of biodiversity for ecological health and stability, ethical considerations emphasize the preservation of species and habitats to maintain ecosystem function.
4. **Interconnectedness:** Ethical perspectives highlight the interconnectedness of all life forms and the role of each species in maintaining ecosystem balance. Human actions can disrupt this delicate equilibrium.
5. **Future Generations:** Ethical considerations extend to future generations, emphasizing our responsibility to leave a diverse and thriving natural world for future

inhabitants of the planet.

6. **Cultural and Indigenous Values:** Many cultures and indigenous communities have deep spiritual, cultural, and traditional connections to wildlife. Respecting these values is essential for ethical decision-making.

Ethical Dilemmas and Solutions:

1. **Conservation vs. Economic Development:** Balancing economic development with conservation efforts often poses ethical dilemmas. Sustainable practices that minimize negative impacts on wildlife and ecosystems are a potential solution.
2. **Wildlife Tourism:** While wildlife tourism can raise awareness and funding for conservation, it can also disrupt animal behaviors and habitats. Responsible and ethical wildlife tourism practices are crucial.
3. **Wildlife Rehabilitation:** Ethical considerations arise when deciding whether to rehabilitate and release individual animals or prioritize conservation efforts for entire populations.
4. **Conflict with Humans:** Managing human-wildlife conflicts requires ethical decisions that consider both human livelihoods and wildlife welfare.

Conclusion:

Human impact on wildlife raises important ethical considerations that require a thoughtful and balanced approach to conservation. Recognizing the intrinsic value of all species, understanding our responsibilities as stewards of the planet, and considering the long-term well-being of ecosystems are central to addressing these challenges ethically and responsibly. Through collaboration, education, and ethical decision-making, humans can strive to coexist with wildlife while minimizing our negative impact on the natural world.

Marine Life: Underwater Wonders

Marine Life: Underwater Wonders

The world's oceans are teeming with a diverse array of marine life, making them some of the most fascinating and diverse ecosystems on Earth. From the smallest plankton to the largest whales, marine life showcases an incredible variety of species and adaptations that have evolved to thrive in the aquatic environment. Exploring marine life not only unveils the wonders of the deep sea but also emphasizes the importance of ocean conservation for the health of our planet.

Diversity of Marine Life:

1. **Microscopic Life:** Phytoplankton and zooplankton are the foundation of marine food chains. These microscopic organisms play a crucial role in nutrient cycling and oxygen production.
2. **Fish and Sharks:** The oceans are home to an immense variety of fish species, ranging from the colorful clownfish to the apex predator great white shark. Fish have evolved an array of adaptations for life underwater, including streamlined bodies and specialized sensory organs.
3. **Marine Mammals:** Dolphins, whales, seals, and sea lions are mammals that have evolved to live in the marine environment. Their adaptations include blubber for insulation, efficient diving abilities, and sophisticated communication systems.
4. **Corals and Coral Reefs:** Coral reefs are among the most biodiverse ecosystems on the planet, providing habitat

for countless species. Corals are tiny animals that form symbiotic relationships with algae, which provide them with energy through photosynthesis.

5. **Invertebrates:** Marine invertebrates include creatures like jellyfish, squid, octopuses, and crustaceans. These animals exhibit unique body structures and behaviors adapted to their underwater habitats.

Adaptations to the Marine Environment:

1. **Buoyancy:** Many marine animals have adaptations for buoyancy, allowing them to stay afloat in the water. This includes air sacs in fish and specialized structures in marine mammals.
2. **Camouflage and Coloration:** Marine animals have developed various camouflage and coloration strategies to blend in with their surroundings, helping them avoid predators and ambush prey.
3. **Echolocation:** Dolphins and some whales use echolocation to navigate and locate prey in the vast ocean depths by emitting sound waves and analyzing the echoes.
4. **Bioluminescence:** Some marine organisms, like certain species of fish and deep-sea creatures, are capable of producing their own light through bioluminescence, which serves functions such as attracting mates and deterring predators.
5. **Salt Tolerance:** Marine animals have evolved mechanisms to cope with high salt concentrations in their environment, including specialized glands to excrete excess salt.

Marine Conservation Challenges:

1. **Overfishing:** Unsustainable fishing practices have led to the depletion of fish populations and disruption of marine food webs.

2. **Coral Bleaching:** Rising sea temperatures due to climate change lead to coral bleaching, where corals expel their symbiotic algae, causing them to lose their color and vitality.
3. **Pollution:** Marine pollution from plastic waste, chemicals, and oil spills poses a grave threat to marine life and ecosystems.
4. **Habitat Destruction:** Coastal development, coral mining, and other human activities threaten the habitats essential for marine species' survival.

Importance of Marine Conservation:

1. **Biodiversity:** Marine ecosystems harbor incredible biodiversity, contributing to ecological stability and providing genetic resources for potential medical and scientific discoveries.
2. **Economic Value:** Fisheries, tourism, and other industries depend on healthy marine ecosystems for economic livelihoods.
3. **Climate Regulation:** Oceans play a vital role in regulating global climate through heat absorption and carbon dioxide storage.

Conclusion:

Exploring marine life reveals the astonishing beauty and complexity of underwater ecosystems. From the smallest organisms to the largest marine mammals, each species contributes to the delicate balance of marine ecosystems. Understanding and conserving marine life are critical for the well-being of both these extraordinary creatures and the planet as a whole.

Coral reefs, marine mammals, and ocean ecosystems

Coral Reefs, Marine Mammals, and Ocean Ecosystems

The world's oceans are home to a remarkable array of ecosystems and species, each playing a crucial role in maintaining the health and balance of our planet. Coral reefs, marine mammals, and ocean ecosystems are interconnected components of these watery worlds, each with unique characteristics and significance.

Coral Reefs: Underwater Rainforests

1. **Biodiversity Hotspots:** Coral reefs are often referred to as the "rainforests of the sea" due to their high biodiversity. They are home to a stunning variety of marine life, from colorful coral polyps to intricate fish species.

2. **Symbiotic Relationships:** Coral reefs thrive through the symbiotic relationship between coral polyps and photosynthetic algae called zooxanthellae. These algae provide energy through photosynthesis, supporting the growth and health of the corals.

3. **Ecosystem Services:** Coral reefs provide essential ecosystem services, including coastal protection from storms, shoreline stabilization, and nurseries for various fish species.

4. **Threats and Conservation:** Coral reefs face threats such as coral bleaching, pollution, overfishing, and climate change. Conservation efforts aim to protect

and restore these fragile ecosystems for future generations.

Marine Mammals: Masters of the Ocean

1. **Adaptations to Aquatic Life:** Marine mammals have evolved a range of adaptations to life in the ocean, such as streamlined bodies, blubber for insulation, and specialized breathing mechanisms.
2. **Communication and Intelligence:** Dolphins, whales, and seals exhibit complex communication and social behaviors. Some species are known for their high levels of intelligence and problem-solving abilities.
3. **Migration and Navigation:** Many marine mammals undertake epic migrations across vast ocean expanses, relying on navigational cues such as Earth's magnetic field, sun position, and underwater sound patterns.
4. **Conservation and Threats:** Marine mammals face threats from habitat loss, pollution, climate change, and accidental entanglement in fishing gear. Conservation efforts include protected areas and regulations to minimize human impact.

Ocean Ecosystems: Interconnected Web of Life

1. **Food Webs:** Ocean ecosystems are complex food webs where species interact and depend on each other for survival. Phytoplankton form the base of these webs, with predators and prey interlinked in intricate relationships.
2. **Nutrient Cycling:** Ocean currents play a crucial role in nutrient cycling, distributing nutrients and supporting the productivity of marine ecosystems.
3. **Biodiversity and Ecological Balance:** Biodiversity in ocean ecosystems promotes ecological balance, ensuring that no single species dominates and that the health of the entire system is maintained.

4. **Threats and Conservation:** Pollution, overfishing, habitat destruction, and climate change pose significant threats to ocean ecosystems. Conservation efforts aim to protect marine biodiversity and restore damaged habitats.

Interconnectedness and Impact:

Coral reefs, marine mammals, and ocean ecosystems are intimately connected, influencing and depending on each other for survival. Healthy coral reefs provide habitats and feeding grounds for marine mammals, while marine mammals play roles in nutrient cycling and predator-prey interactions that affect overall ecosystem health. Understanding and protecting these elements of ocean life are essential for the preservation of our planet's biodiversity and the well-being of future generations.

Threats to marine life and coral reef conservation

Threats to Marine Life and Coral Reef Conservation

Marine life and coral reefs, vital components of Earth's ecosystems, face a multitude of threats that endanger their health and survival. Coral reef conservation efforts are crucial to mitigate these threats and protect the delicate balance of underwater ecosystems.

1. Climate Change:

- **Coral Bleaching:** Rising sea temperatures cause coral bleaching, where corals expel the symbiotic algae that give them color and nutrients. Bleaching weakens corals and makes them susceptible to disease and death.

2. Ocean Acidification:

- **Carbon Dioxide Absorption:** Oceans absorb excess carbon dioxide from the atmosphere, leading to higher acidity levels. This inhibits the ability of marine organisms, especially coral polyps, to build their calcium carbonate skeletons.

3. Overfishing and Destructive Fishing Practices:

- **Unsustainable Fishing:** Overfishing depletes fish populations, disrupts food chains, and affects the balance of marine ecosystems. Destructive methods like dynamite fishing and bottom trawling harm coral reefs and habitats.

4. Pollution:

- **Runoff and Chemicals:** Agricultural runoff, sewage, and industrial pollutants can lead to nutrient pollution and the spread of harmful chemicals in marine environments.

5. Coastal Development:

- **Habitat Destruction:** Coastal development, including tourism infrastructure and urbanization, can lead to habitat destruction, sedimentation, and pollution.

6. Invasive Species:

- **Non-Native Species:** Invasive species can outcompete native species for resources and disrupt the natural balance of marine ecosystems.

7. Unsustainable Tourism:

- **Coral Damage:** Unregulated tourism, especially through practices like anchor dropping, can cause physical damage to coral reefs and disturb marine life.

8. Dynamite Fishing and Coral Mining:

- **Habitat Destruction:** Dynamite fishing and coral mining for construction materials lead to direct destruction of coral reefs, severely impacting their ecosystems.

Coral Reef Conservation Efforts:

Coral reef conservation aims to address these threats and protect these vital ecosystems:

- **Marine Protected Areas:** Establishing protected areas helps restrict fishing, prevent damage, and allow recovery of coral reefs.

- **Sustainable Fishing Practices:** Implementing regulations and practices that limit fishing pressure and protect critical species.
- **Coral Restoration:** Initiatives involve growing and transplanting corals to degraded areas to help them recover.
- **Education and Awareness:** Educating communities and tourists about the importance of coral reefs fosters responsible behavior and reduces human impact.
- **Climate Change Mitigation:** Addressing climate change through global efforts to reduce greenhouse gas emissions is essential to protect coral reefs and marine life.

Coral reef conservation requires international cooperation, local engagement, and a commitment to preserving the beauty, biodiversity, and ecological services these underwater wonders provide to our planet.

Sustainable practices for marine environment preservation

Sustainable Practices for Marine Environment Preservation

Preserving the marine environment and its biodiversity requires adopting sustainable practices that balance human needs with the health of oceans and marine ecosystems. Here are some key sustainable practices:

1. Sustainable Fishing:

- **Fisheries Management:** Implement science-based quotas, size limits, and closed seasons to prevent overfishing and ensure fish populations can replenish.
- **Selective Fishing Gear:** Use gear that minimizes bycatch and avoids damaging habitats, such as using hooks instead of trawls.

2. Marine Protected Areas (MPAs):

- **Biodiversity Conservation:** Establish MPAs to protect sensitive marine habitats, breeding grounds, and ecosystems from human activities.
- **No-Take Zones:** Create areas where no fishing is allowed to promote the recovery of fish populations and habitats.

3. Responsible Tourism:

- **Eco-Tourism:** Promote responsible practices that minimize impact on marine ecosystems, such as snorkeling and diving without touching coral reefs.

- **Boating Etiquette:** Educate boaters about avoiding coral reefs, anchoring in designated areas, and avoiding wildlife disturbance.

4. Reduce Plastic Pollution:

- **Plastic-Free Choices:** Reduce single-use plastic consumption, use reusable items, and properly dispose of plastic waste to prevent marine pollution.
- **Beach Cleanups:** Organize and participate in beach cleanups to prevent plastics from entering the oceans.

5. Sustainable Coastal Development:

- **Erosion Control:** Implement erosion control measures to prevent sediment runoff into the oceans, which can smother coral reefs and marine habitats.
- **Sustainable Infrastructure:** Design coastal developments to minimize impact on habitats and water quality.

6. Climate Change Mitigation:

- **Reduce Carbon Footprint:** Adopt energy-efficient practices, use renewable energy sources, and support policies that reduce greenhouse gas emissions.
- **Support Conservation Organizations:** Contribute to organizations working to address climate change and protect marine ecosystems.

7. Support Research and Education:

- **Scientific Research:** Support marine research initiatives that study marine life, habitats, and the impacts of human activities.
- **Education Programs:** Promote marine education and awareness among local communities, schools, and tourists.

8. Responsible Seafood Consumption:

- **Sustainable Seafood:** Choose seafood certified by sustainable seafood organizations that promote responsible fishing practices.
- **Know Your Source:** Be informed about where your seafood comes from to ensure it's sourced responsibly.

9. Reduce Chemical Pollution:

- **Proper Disposal:** Dispose of chemicals, oil, and hazardous waste properly to prevent contamination of marine environments.
- **Use Eco-Friendly Products:** Choose eco-friendly cleaning and personal care products to prevent harmful chemicals from entering the oceans.

10. Participate in Conservation Initiatives:

- **Volunteer and Donate:** Contribute to marine conservation efforts by volunteering for marine-related organizations or donating to support their work.

By embracing these sustainable practices, individuals, communities, and industries can contribute to the preservation of marine ecosystems, ensuring that they remain vibrant, diverse, and resilient for future generations.

Paleontology and Fossils

Paleontology and Fossils

Paleontology is the scientific study of the history of life on Earth through the examination of plant and animal fossils. Fossils are the preserved remains of ancient organisms or traces of their activities that offer valuable insights into Earth's past. Here's an overview of paleontology and fossils:

1. Importance of Fossils:

- **Time Capsules:** Fossils provide a window into the past, revealing the diversity of ancient life forms and the conditions of their environments.
- **Evolutionary Insights:** Fossils help scientists understand the process of evolution, how species have changed over time, and how new species have emerged.
- **Climate and Environment:** Fossilized plants, animals, and ancient landscapes offer clues about past climates, ecosystems, and geological events.
- **Extinction Events:** Fossils help uncover the causes and consequences of mass extinctions, shedding light on the resilience of life on Earth.

2. Fossil Formation:

- **Mineralization:** Minerals replace organic material in bones, shells, and other tissues, preserving their structure.
- **Petrification:** Organic material is replaced by minerals, transforming it into stone-like material.

- **Carbonization:** Soft tissues leave behind a thin layer of carbon after being compressed over time.
- **Trace Fossils:** Impressions, tracks, burrows, and other traces of ancient organisms are preserved in sediments.

3. Types of Fossils:

- **Body Fossils:** Actual remains of organisms, such as bones, teeth, and shells.
- **Mold and Cast Fossils:** Impressions of organisms are left in sediments, which later form casts when minerals fill the cavities.
- **Trace Fossils:** Evidence of the activity of organisms, like footprints, tracks, and burrows.
- **Pollen and Spores:** Plant reproductive structures preserved in sediments.
- **Amber Fossils:** Insects and small organisms preserved in hardened tree resin.

4. Methods of Study:

- **Field Work:** Paleontologists search for fossils in various environments, from deserts to quarries to riverbeds.
- **Excavation:** Fossils are carefully unearthed using tools like brushes, picks, and shovels.
- **Laboratory Analysis:** Fossils are cleaned, examined, and often studied using specialized equipment like microscopes and CT scanners.
- **Comparative Anatomy:** Scientists compare fossilized remains with living organisms to understand their evolutionary relationships.

5. Contributions to Science:

- **Evolutionary Theory:** Fossils provide evidence for the theory of evolution, showcasing the transitions between different species.

- **Geological Time Scale:** Fossils help establish the chronological order of Earth's history and the development of life.
- **Environmental Reconstruction:** Fossilized plants and animals offer insights into ancient ecosystems and habitats.
- **Extinction Patterns:** Fossil records reveal patterns of species extinction and recovery over time.

6. Conservation and Ethical Considerations:

- **Preservation:** Proper handling and storage of fossils are crucial to their preservation for future research.
- **Ethics:** Fossils should be collected ethically and legally, respecting the cultural and scientific value they hold.

7. Popular Fossil Discoveries:

- **Dinosaurs:** Fossils of these ancient reptiles have captured public imagination for their size and diversity.
- **Mammoths and Mastodons:** Ancient relatives of elephants that roamed during the Ice Age.
- **Prehistoric Marine Life:** Fossilized marine organisms like ammonites and trilobites offer insights into ancient oceans.

8. Modern Techniques:

- **CT Scanning:** Non-destructive imaging reveals the internal structures of fossils.
- **DNA Analysis:** In rare cases, preserved DNA offers insights into the genetics of ancient organisms.
- **3D Printing:** Replicas of fossils can be made using 3D printing technology.

Paleontology and the study of fossils continue to provide invaluable knowledge about Earth's history, the evolution of life, and the dynamic interplay between organisms and their environment.

The study of fossils and ancient life forms

The study of fossils and ancient life forms, known as paleontology, is a captivating field that offers a glimpse into the history of life on Earth. Fossils are the preserved remains of once-living organisms or traces of their activities, providing valuable insights into the diversity, behavior, and environments of prehistoric creatures. Here's an exploration of the study of fossils and ancient life forms:

1. Unveiling the Past:

- Fossils serve as "snapshots" of life from different periods in Earth's history, allowing scientists to reconstruct ecosystems, behaviors, and adaptations.
- By studying fossils, paleontologists can piece together the evolutionary history of species, from their origins to their eventual extinction.

2. Fossilization Processes:

- Fossilization occurs through various processes such as mineralization, petrification, and carbonization, which transform organic materials into more durable forms over millions of years.
- Sediments, minerals, and other environmental factors play a role in the preservation of fossils.

3. Types of Fossils:

- Body Fossils: These include the actual preserved remains of organisms such as bones, teeth, and shells.
- Trace Fossils: These capture traces of ancient

organisms' activities, such as footprints, burrows, and nests.

- Coprolites: Fossilized excrement that provides information about the diet and behavior of ancient animals.
- Pollen and Spores: Tiny reproductive structures of plants, preserved in sediment layers, reveal past vegetation and climate.

4. Evolutionary Insights:

- Fossils provide direct evidence of the changes that have occurred in various species over time, showcasing evolutionary transitions and adaptations.
- Transitional fossils, such as Tiktaalik, offer a bridge between different groups of organisms, shedding light on the evolutionary process.

5. Paleoenvironments and Paleoecology:

- Fossils provide information about ancient environments, such as the climate, geography, and ecosystems that existed millions of years ago.
- By studying the interactions between ancient organisms and their environments, paleontologists can reconstruct entire ecosystems.

6. Evolution of Behaviors:

- Fossil evidence can reveal behavioral traits of ancient organisms, including feeding habits, locomotion, and social interactions.
- Trackways and burrows provide insights into the movement and behavior of prehistoric animals.

7. Mass Extinctions:

- The fossil record holds clues about mass extinctions, including the causes, consequences, and subsequent recoveries of life.

- The K-T extinction event, associated with the demise of the dinosaurs, is one of the most well-known examples.

8. Modern Techniques:

- Technological advancements, such as high-resolution imaging and computed tomography (CT) scanning, allow researchers to examine fossils in detail without damaging them.
- Isotope analysis helps determine the diet, habitat, and movement patterns of ancient organisms.

9. Ethics and Conservation:

- Collecting fossils responsibly and ethically is essential to preserving these valuable scientific resources.
- Many countries have regulations and guidelines to ensure the proper collection and preservation of fossils.

10. Education and Outreach:

- Fossils capture the public's imagination and play a significant role in science education and outreach efforts.
- Museums, educational programs, and documentaries showcase fossils and their importance in understanding Earth's history.

From the towering dinosaurs of the Mesozoic Era to the microscopic fossils of ancient microorganisms, the study of fossils and ancient life forms offers a unique and compelling window into the past, enabling us to unravel the mysteries of our planet's history and the evolution of life.

Notable fossil discoveries and their significance

Throughout the history of paleontology, there have been several notable fossil discoveries that have had a significant impact on our understanding of ancient life, evolution, and the history of the Earth. Here are some of the most remarkable and significant fossil discoveries:

1. **Archaeopteryx:** Discovered in Germany in the 1860s, Archaeopteryx is often referred to as the "first bird." This fossil has both bird-like and reptile-like features, providing key evidence for the link between dinosaurs and modern birds. It showcases the transition from terrestrial dinosaurs to avian flight.

2. **Tiktaalik:** Found in Canada's Arctic in 2004, Tiktaalik is an intermediate fossil between fish and tetrapods (four-limbed vertebrates). Its well-preserved limbs with finger-like bones indicate the transition from aquatic to terrestrial environments during the evolution of land animals.

3. **Lucy (Australopithecus afarensis):** Discovered in Ethiopia in 1974, the fossilized remains of Lucy are one of the most famous hominid fossils. This partial skeleton belongs to the species Australopithecus afarensis and provided crucial insights into the early stages of human evolution, including bipedalism.

4. **Tyrannosaurus rex:** The discovery of the Tyrannosaurus rex fossil in the late 19th century in North America captured public imagination. T. rex is one of the most iconic dinosaurs, and

its fossils have contributed to our understanding of dinosaur anatomy, behavior, and the Cretaceous period.

5. Homo naledi: Discovered in a South African cave in 2013, the fossils of Homo naledi represent a previously unknown species of hominin. This discovery challenges our understanding of human evolution, as the species exhibits both primitive and advanced features.

6. Ida (Darwinius masillae): Unveiled in 2009, Ida is a remarkably preserved primate fossil from Germany. While it generated excitement for being dubbed the "missing link," its position in the evolutionary tree has been debated. Nonetheless, it highlighted the importance of well-preserved specimens for research.

7. Anomalocaris: Anomalocaris, a bizarre marine creature from the Cambrian period, was initially described in the 19th century. However, its true identity was debated until the discovery of well-preserved specimens in Canada's Burgess Shale. It played a role in reconstructing the Cambrian explosion and ancient marine ecosystems.

8. Sue (Tyrannosaurus rex): Sue is one of the most complete and well-preserved T. rex skeletons ever found. Discovered in South Dakota in 1990, the fossil provided insights into the anatomy, growth, and lifestyle of this apex predator.

9. Coelacanth: Once thought to be extinct, the coelacanth was discovered alive off the coast of South Africa in 1938. Fossils of coelacanths date back to the Devonian period, making them a "living fossil" that provides insights into ancient fish evolution.

10. Ichthyosaur Fossils: The discovery of ichthyosaur fossils in the 19th century helped scientists understand the diversity of marine reptiles in the Mesozoic era. These fossils showed the adaptation of reptiles to a marine lifestyle and contributed to our understanding of ancient marine ecosystems.

These are just a few examples of the many significant fossil discoveries that have shaped our understanding of Earth's history and the evolution of life. Each discovery provides a window into the past and contributes to our ongoing quest to unravel the mysteries of ancient life and the natural world.

Contributions of paleontology to understanding Earth's history

Paleontology, the study of fossils and ancient life, has made significant contributions to our understanding of Earth's history by providing insights into the past environments, ecosystems, and evolutionary processes. Here are some key contributions of paleontology to understanding Earth's history:

1. **Evolution of Life:** Fossils document the evolutionary history of life on Earth, revealing the gradual changes in species over millions of years. By studying fossils, paleontologists can trace the origins of different groups of organisms, their diversification, and the relationships between species.

2. **Geologic Time Scale:** Fossil evidence is crucial for constructing the geologic time scale, which divides Earth's history into distinct eras, periods, and epochs. The arrangement of fossils in sedimentary rock layers allows scientists to date events in Earth's past and understand the sequence of biological and geological changes.

3. **Mass Extinctions:** Fossils provide evidence of past mass extinctions, such as the Permian-Triassic and Cretaceous-Paleogene extinctions. These events had profound impacts on Earth's ecosystems and shaped the course of evolution by creating opportunities for new species to emerge.

4. **Climate Change:** Fossils of plants, animals, and microorganisms from different time periods offer

insights into past climates and environmental conditions. By studying the types of organisms present and their adaptations, scientists can reconstruct ancient ecosystems and track changes in temperature, sea levels, and atmospheric composition.

5. **Plate Tectonics:** Fossil distributions across continents provide evidence for continental drift and the movement of tectonic plates. Similar fossils found on continents that are now widely separated suggest that these landmasses were once connected.

6. **Ancient Environments:** Fossils help reconstruct ancient terrestrial and aquatic environments. By studying the types of organisms found in a particular area, scientists can infer factors such as temperature, humidity, and the presence of water bodies.

7. **Origin of Life:** Paleontology contributes to the study of the origin of life by providing evidence of early microbial life forms and the conditions under which they existed. Fossils of microbial mats and stromatolites offer clues about Earth's earliest ecosystems.

8. **Biogeography:** Fossils help explain the distribution of organisms across different continents and regions. Similar fossil assemblages in different parts of the world can indicate past connections between landmasses or the movement of species.

9. **Human Evolution:** The study of hominin fossils has provided insights into the evolution of humans and our ancestors. Fossil evidence reveals the emergence of bipedalism, brain size changes, and the development of tools and culture.

10. **Preservation of Soft Tissues:** In some exceptional cases, paleontology has uncovered fossils with preserved soft tissues, providing insights into the anatomy, behavior, and even coloration of ancient organisms.

Overall, paleontology plays a crucial role in piecing together Earth's history and the story of life's evolution. Fossils provide a direct window into the past, allowing scientists to reconstruct ancient ecosystems, understand evolutionary processes, and uncover the mysteries of the natural world.

Celebrating the Richness of Animal Kingdom

The animal kingdom is a vast and diverse realm that encompasses a breathtaking array of species, each uniquely adapted to its environment and way of life. From the smallest insects to the largest mammals, the world of animals is a testament to the wonders of evolution and the complexity of life itself. Celebrating the richness of the animal kingdom allows us to marvel at the beauty, ingenuity, and diversity that exists within our natural world.

In the depths of the oceans, graceful marine creatures glide through the water, while on land, mammals roam the savannahs and forests with remarkable agility. Birds take to the skies in a symphony of colors and melodies, showcasing their incredible adaptations for flight. From the smallest of creatures like ants and bees that work tirelessly in intricate societies, to the majestic predators like lions and tigers that rule their domains, the animal kingdom is a stage where every species plays a vital role.

This celebration isn't just about admiration; it's also about recognizing the importance of these creatures in maintaining the delicate balance of ecosystems. Biodiversity, the variety of life on Earth, ensures that each species has a unique role in contributing to ecosystem functions, such as pollination, nutrient cycling, and predator-prey interactions. The interconnectedness of species highlights the intricate web of life that sustains us all.

Moreover, studying the animal kingdom unlocks the mysteries of adaptation, survival, and evolution. From the camouflaged insects that blend seamlessly into their surroundings to the incredible migrations undertaken by certain species, animals have developed ingenious strategies to thrive in their environments. Learning about their behaviors, communication methods, and reproductive strategies provides valuable insights into the ways life has evolved to conquer challenges and seize opportunities.

In this celebration, we also acknowledge the ongoing efforts to protect and conserve the animal kingdom. Habitat loss, climate change, pollution, and overexploitation threaten many species with extinction. Conservation initiatives, research, and education are essential for ensuring that future generations can continue to marvel at the wonders of the animal kingdom.

As we celebrate the richness of the animal kingdom, let us foster a deep respect for all creatures, big and small. Whether it's a captivating insect, a majestic predator, or a delicate sea creature, each has a story to tell and a role to play. By understanding and valuing the diversity of life on our planet, we honor the intricate tapestry of existence that has evolved over millions of years.

Reflection on the diversity and wonder of animals

The diversity and wonder of animals on our planet is truly awe-inspiring. From the tiniest insects to the largest mammals, the variety of species and the incredible adaptations they have developed to survive and thrive in their environments is a testament to the beauty and complexity of life on Earth.

As we delve into the world of animals, we encounter an astonishing array of forms, behaviors, and ecological niches. The colors and patterns of butterflies' wings, the intricate social structures of primates, the stealth and strength of big cats, the graceful movements of marine creatures – each aspect of the animal kingdom tells a unique story of evolution and adaptation.

The more we learn about animals, the more we realize that their lives are filled with extraordinary behaviors, complex interactions, and astonishing abilities. The intricate dance of honeybees as they communicate the location of nectar, the elaborate courtship rituals of birds, the navigational feats of migrating whales – these glimpses into the lives of animals reveal a world of intricacy and intelligence.

The study of animals also fosters a deep appreciation for the interconnectedness of ecosystems and the delicate balance of nature. Each species, no matter how small or seemingly insignificant, plays a role in maintaining the health and stability of its habitat. The disappearance of a single species can have far-reaching consequences that ripple through entire ecosystems.

Beyond their scientific significance, animals hold a special place in our hearts and cultures. They inspire us with their beauty, courage, and resilience. They provide companionship, service, and inspiration to humans in ways that have shaped our societies and even our own evolution.

As we reflect on the diversity and wonder of animals, we are reminded of our responsibility to protect and conserve the world's precious biodiversity. The alarming rate of species extinction due to human activities underscores the urgency of our role as stewards of the Earth. Our choices and actions will determine the fate of countless species and the ecosystems they inhabit.

Ultimately, the exploration of the animal kingdom invites us to marvel at the mysteries of life itself. It invites us to celebrate the incredible diversity of creatures that share our planet and to recognize the interconnectedness of all living beings. Through understanding and valuing the world of animals, we gain insights into the rich tapestry of life and our place within it.

The importance of continued exploration and conservation

Continued exploration and conservation of the animal kingdom are of paramount importance for the well-being of both our planet and future generations. The intricate web of life that exists on Earth is a delicate balance, where each species plays a role in maintaining the health and stability of ecosystems. As we learn more about animals and their interactions, we gain valuable insights into the complex relationships that sustain life on our planet.

Exploration drives scientific discovery and innovation. By studying animals, we unlock secrets about their behavior, physiology, genetics, and adaptations. These insights not only deepen our understanding of the natural world but also have practical applications in fields such as medicine, technology, and conservation biology. For example, the study of animal behavior has led to advancements in understanding human psychology, while biomimicry – drawing inspiration from nature's designs – has inspired innovations in engineering and materials science.

Conservation is crucial to protect the incredible biodiversity of the animal kingdom. Many animal species are currently facing threats such as habitat loss, pollution, climate change, and overexploitation. The loss of a single species can disrupt entire ecosystems, leading to cascading effects on other species and the environment as a whole. Conservation efforts aim to prevent these losses and maintain the health and functioning of ecosystems for future generations.

Furthermore, animals have an intrinsic value that goes beyond their utility to humans. Every species has evolved over millions of years, adapting to its unique environment and contributing to the intricate tapestry of life. Each species represents a unique branch in the tree of life, and the extinction of even one species is a loss of biodiversity that can never be recovered. The extinction of a species also represents the loss of potential benefits to future generations, from scientific discoveries to potential solutions to environmental challenges.

Conservation efforts can also have positive ripple effects for human communities. Healthy ecosystems provide services such as clean air and water, pollination of crops, and natural resources. Conserving wildlife habitats can contribute to ecotourism and sustainable livelihoods for local communities.

In conclusion, continued exploration and conservation of the animal kingdom are essential for the well-being of our planet, the advancement of scientific knowledge, and the preservation of biodiversity. By valuing and protecting the incredible diversity of animals, we ensure a sustainable future for both the natural world and human society. Our collective efforts can make a significant difference in safeguarding the beauty and complexity of life on Earth.

Definitions and explanations of scientific terms used throughout the book

Throughout "The World of Animals: A Comprehensive Guide," readers will encounter a wide range of scientific terms that help describe the diverse world of animals. Here are some key terms and explanations to aid in understanding the content:

1. **Taxonomy**: The science of classifying and categorizing organisms based on their evolutionary relationships, encompassing various levels such as domain, kingdom, phylum, class, order, family, genus, and species.
2. **Habitat**: The natural environment or location where an organism lives, including all the biotic and abiotic factors that influence its survival.
3. **Adaptation**: A characteristic or trait that has evolved in an organism over time to help it survive and reproduce in its environment.
4. **Biodiversity**: The variety and variability of life forms present in a particular ecosystem, habitat, or on Earth as a whole.
5. **Ecosystem**: A complex community of living organisms (plants, animals, microorganisms) and their physical environment, interacting as a functional unit.
6. **Extinction**: The complete disappearance of a species from the Earth, often due to environmental changes, habitat loss, predation, or human activities.
7. **Conservation**: The management and protection of natural resources, ecosystems, and wildlife to

prevent extinction, maintain biodiversity, and ensure sustainable use.

8. **Behavior**: Observable actions or responses of organisms to their environment, including various activities like feeding, mating, communication, and movement.

9. **Domestication**: The process by which wild animals or plants are tamed and bred for human use and purposes, resulting in genetic changes over generations.

10. **Metamorphosis**: A process of developmental change in insects and some amphibians, involving distinct stages like egg, larva, pupa, and adult.

11. **Carnivore**: An animal that primarily eats other animals for sustenance, characterized by sharp teeth and a digestive system adapted for a meat-based diet.

12. **Herbivore**: An animal that primarily feeds on plants and vegetation, with specialized adaptations for extracting nutrients from plant material.

13. **Omnivore**: An animal that consumes both plant matter and other animals, often possessing a versatile diet and digestive system.

14. **Ecosystem Services**: The benefits that humans receive from ecosystems, including functions like pollination, water purification, soil fertility, and carbon sequestration.

15. **Endangered Species**: A species that is at risk of becoming extinct due to declining population numbers and ongoing threats to its survival.

16. **Invasive Species**: Non-native species that are introduced to a new ecosystem and can cause harm to the environment, economy, or human health.

17. **Keystone Species**: A species that has a disproportionately large impact on its ecosystem relative to its abundance, influencing the structure and diversity of the community.

18. **Predation**: The act of one organism (predator) killing and consuming another organism (prey) for food.
19. **Symbiosis**: A close interaction between two different species, often involving mutualistic, commensal, or parasitic relationships.
20. **Territorial Behavior**: The defense and control of a specific area by an animal or group of animals, often for resources like food, mates, or nesting sites.

These are just a few examples of the scientific terms that readers may encounter while exploring the world of animals in the book. Understanding these terms is essential for grasping the concepts and principles that underlie the fascinating and diverse behaviors, adaptations, and interactions of animals across the globe.

Suggested books, websites, and references for further exploration

For readers interested in further exploring the captivating world of animals, here are some suggested books, websites, and references that offer in-depth information and insights:

Books:

1. "The Princeton Field Guide to Dinosaurs" by Gregory S. Paul
2. "The Hidden Life of Trees: What They Feel, How They Communicate" by Peter Wohlleben
3. "The Soul of an Octopus: A Surprising Exploration into the Wonder of Consciousness" by Sy Montgomery
4. "The Genius of Birds" by Jennifer Ackerman
5. "The Sixth Extinction: An Unnatural History" by Elizabeth Kolbert
6. "The Secret Wisdom of Nature: Trees, Animals, and the Extraordinary Balance of All Living Things - Stories from Science and Observation" by Peter Wohlleben

Websites and Online Resources:

1. National Geographic's Animals: Offers a wealth of information on a wide range of animal species, their behaviors, habitats, and conservation efforts. Website: www.nationalgeographic.com/animals/
2. Smithsonian's National Museum of Natural History: Provides educational resources, exhibitions, and research updates on various animal topics. Website:

naturalhistory.si.edu

3. Animal Diversity Web: Hosted by the University of Michigan Museum of Zoology, this database offers detailed information on animal species, including photos, videos, and taxonomy. Website: animaldiversity.org
4. The Cornell Lab of Ornithology: Focuses on bird species and offers resources for birdwatching, identification, and conservation efforts. Website: www.birds.cornell.edu
5. The International Union for Conservation of Nature (IUCN): Provides information on species conservation status, threats, and action plans. Website: www.iucn.org

Scientific Journals and Publications:

1. "Animal Behaviour": A journal that publishes research on animal behavior, covering topics such as ecology, evolution, and cognition. Website: www.journals.elsevier.com/animal-behaviour/
2. "Zoological Journal of the Linnean Society": Publishes research related to animal taxonomy, systematics, and evolution. Website: academic.oup.com/zoolinnean
3. "Conservation Biology": Focuses on the study and preservation of biodiversity and the environment. Website: conbio.onlinelibrary.wiley.com/journal/15231739
4. "Marine Ecology Progress Series": Publishes research on marine ecosystems, including marine life and conservation. Website: www.int-res.com/journals/meps/

These resources offer a comprehensive and enriching journey into the diverse and fascinating realm of animals. Whether you're interested in dinosaurs, marine life, animal behavior, or conservation efforts, these books, websites, and publications provide valuable insights and knowledge for curious minds.